NO ORDINARY GAME

NO ORDINARY GAME

Miraculous Moments in
Backyards and Sandlots

Kirk Westphal

Kirk Westphal
2017

Down East Books

Camden, Maine

Published by Down East Books
A wholly owned subsidiary of The Rowman & Littlefield Publishing Group, Inc.
4501 Forbes Boulevard, Suite 200, Lanham, Maryland 20706
www.rowman.com

Unit A, Whitacre Mews, 26-34 Stannary Street, London SE11 4AB

Distributed by National Book Network

British Library Cataloguing in Publication Information Available

Library of Congress Cataloging-in-Publication Data Available

ISBN 978-1-60893-363-1 (pbk. : alk. paper)
ISBN 978-1-60893-364-8 (electronic)

♾™ The paper used in this publication meets the minimum requirements of
American National Standard for Information Sciences Permanence of Paper for
Printed Library Materials, ANSI/NISO Z39.48-1992.

Printed in the United States of America

For Ben and Ellie
Keep playing, my friends

CONTENTS

PROLOGUE

I was raised on the shores of Lake Michigan as a Cubs fan. Of my formative boyhood lessons, I learned decency, inquiry, and responsibility from my parents, and the celebration of life from Harry Caray. I knew every player, every year: Rick Monday, Keith Moreland, Ron Cey, Leon Durham, Ryne Sandberg, Dave Kingman, Bruce Sutter, Rick Ruschel, Rick Sutcliffe, Lee Smith. Every summer, my father would load our eager family into the car and drive us from the southwest corner of Michigan to the north side of Chicago. We would walk past the sidewalk vendors, sometimes stopping to purchase a new cap or a team photo, sometimes pausing just long enough to smell the hot dogs. Through the gates and down the concourse, we would catch ephemeral glimpses of the emerald-green world that lay within the friendly confines, and finally, we would ascend the girdered ramps and stairways into the grandstand. In the span of one second my field of view would dissolve from the disarray of people and metal and concrete and more people to the expansive symmetry of a baseball diamond, its oddly alluring flatness, and the unwavering perfection of its colors: dust-brown earth, gleaming white lines and bases, and green so lustrous as to make all other colors beholden to it.

Back then, you could bring your own food into the ballpark, and we would fill an entire plastic garbage bag with day-old buttered popcorn, quite possibly the most exquisite cuisine of the Western world, if you like baseball. We always had good seats at Wrigley Field, usually just beyond first or third base in the grandstands. All of the games were day games back then. My childhood coincided with the great revolt in the north side during which most residents within ten blocks of the ballpark posted signs in their windows that barked "No Lights in Wrigley!" It was a good time to be a young boy, despite the fact that my heroes were better known as the doormats of the National League.

When the time came for me to bid farewell to my family and set off to college, I traveled east to Boston, where I have lived most of my life since. To spend time in Boston without developing feelings for the Red Sox is to spend a day on the beach without getting wet, tanned, or burnt. Not everybody enjoys baseball, but only those with stunted humanity can live here without developing affinity, passion, empathy, or perhaps just allegorical kinship to the Red Sox. Before 2004, they represented the struggle for the unattainable with the hope that it might be attained. It is perhaps a condemnation to spend a life as both a Cubs and Red Sox fan. Surely, the fundamental rights endowed by my Creator have been violated, or are at least not as self-evident as they might have been.

As a boy in Michigan, I had befriended a younger neighborhood boy who had moved from Boston and had brought his Red Sox passion with him. How, I wondered, could any team but the Cubs evoke so much angst and exhilaration in the same inning? I would not understand until I saw my first game at Fenway Park. It was to be the first of many; games in the outfield bleachers, games against the Yankees, a game in the snow with rooftop seats, games with my children, a game with my father—his first game at Fenway—my *thank you* for the Cubs games.

The dreams of a boy change very little as they age. There was even a summer in which a college friend worked as a nighttime security guard at Fenway and would sneak us into the ballpark at night to let us run around the bases and hit fly balls into the dark and listen to hear if they banged off the hallowed Green Monster. He was caught a few months later and promptly fired, but we will forever have that immortal notch in our imaginary dugout wall. I have to admit that while my heart still pounds with zeal, dread, and lust for redemption whenever the Cubs trot out onto the field, my boyhood passion for them has diminished just slightly with the distance, and I have grown particularly fond of the roustabouts who ply their trade in the shadows of Fenway Park. My father accuses me of heresy for dividing my allegiances, but his ground is shaky— he and my mother have since moved to New York, and he has become one of the Bronx faithful.

Needless to say, I have lived most of my life unaccustomed to favorable highlight reels, pennants flapping in the breeze, or, of course, championships. Allocating my most fervent allegiances to the Cubs and Red Sox was like investing my life savings in the Titanic and the Tacoma Narrows Bridge, with the exception that the sinking and the shaking repeat themselves year after year after year. Granted, the Red Sox have provided some measure of redemption since 2004, but I decided to write this book in the hope that I could find highlights, championships, and impossible comebacks in more common venues, perhaps right in front of me all along. I was surprised at what I remembered and what I discovered.

My children have helped with this a bit, to their everlasting credit. At age seven, my daughter was the only girl in her grade playing Little League baseball with the boys, and she struck out the biggest, strongest kid in the league on the afternoon of her pitching debut. Her subtle fist pump and twinkle in her eye as she looked over at me in the dugout erased many of my own frailties. And my son, later that year at age eleven, arced a game-winning goal into the upper right corner of the soccer net as time expired, from fifty feet away. The jubilance of his bouncing teammates transformed the shoddy field atop an old landfill into a megalithic Olympic stadium.

As they showed, a grand stage is not a requisite setting for a great moment. Indeed, victory itself is only an occasional ingredient. I believe that just about anybody could have written the accounts that follow. They are of everyday events that shine with just a little more than the usual luster. They happen to everybody all the time, but to each of us only a handful of times, if we're lucky. This collection of stories didn't arise from the hard-court or the diamond or the gridiron, but rather from the sand lots, asphalt, and chain-link fences that host America's pickup games and recreational leagues. The events in this book are not great by the usual standards of sports literature, but they are great to me simply because they happened . . . to me, or in front of me, and in the process of happening and being remembered, theirs became a stage as grand as any.

Every year there are probably hundreds of thousands of games sponsored by recreational leagues, intramural leagues, or just by the players who happen upon each other at an opportune time. These games are not recorded, their statistics are not counted, and many are not even officiated. They come and go with the daylight and disperse with the players. But they matter, and once in a while, an everyday game transcends itself and becomes embossed in the sublime sporting history shared only by its players. Over my lifetime of forty-five years, I have played and coached thousands of unofficial games: variations of baseball, basketball, football, soccer, and hockey. The number of indelible moments is in the single digits.

Yet these moments were truly formative, and whatever character I may claim to present to the world around me was influenced in some way by these events and by these people. The chapters that follow are the record of uncommon moments in my life as a decidedly amateur athlete and coach. They may be very familiar.

1

HOME COURT ADVANTAGE

I am on an outbound train from New York City on a midsummer evening. A heat wave that has smothered the East Coast for a week broke earlier this afternoon. The train is passing by Coop City, the projects, and people who have finished supper are outside for some refreshingly cool evening air. The train has already traveled past Manhattan, past the Empire State Building, the Chrysler Building, the Triboro Bridge . . . the icons of their city. But the one that catches my eye this evening, for the brief moment that it fills the window of my coach car, is one shared by cities all over the United States, yet particularly symbolic of the character of New York. It is an outdoor basketball court on a summer evening. It is filled with teenage boys playing five-on-five, and dozens of others waiting around the sidelines for the next game. Basketball on asphalt in the city in the summer is urban Americana. It is a vitalizing experience for anyone whose walk of life doesn't normally pass through urban America, and for anyone who plays competitive basketball, an opportunity not to be missed. I had my opportunity . . . just once.

I attended college in Boston in the late 1980s, when the Red Sox were recovering from 1986, the Patriots were recovering from the

Chicago Bears, and long before Ray Borque would bring the Stanley Cup back to Boston . . . as a member of the Colorado Avalanche. But the Celtics were coming off the crest of Larry Bird, Kevin McHale, and Robert Parrish, and so I chose basketball as my pastime when classes weren't in session, and quite frequently, even when they were. I had played once in a while when I was in high school, with friends, with my father, or alone in my driveway. But in college, I played basketball competitively almost every day and had the shin splints and recurring shoulder dislocations to prove it. It was not so much an obsession as it was simply a part of the daily routine and a way to blow off academic steam without offending the faculty. I played in the gyms at a school with over twenty-thousand students, and I knew where the good games would be. I intentionally sought out the courts that drew the guys who had played high school ball, and playing with them coached me in the dynamics of the game, the elements beyond the fundamentals of dribbling and shooting and passing and keeping your eyes on your man's hips when you're defending. I remember learning the effectiveness of a pick at the age of nineteen as I struggled to reclaim my wind. It was a good lesson. I learned how to play a zone defense, though penetrating a zone with the ball completely flummoxed me. I learned how to block shots and when not to try. I learned the give and go, the pick and roll, and the drive and kick, which, as it turns out, can be an effective way to beat the zone. I learned how to play the baseline on both sides of the ball. I developed a turnaround fadeaway baseline jump shot to compensate for my vertical ineptitude, and this became the one skill that I could actually boast about—it was my money shot. To a kid whose sporting life had thus far been devoted to following the wallowing of the Chicago

Cubs, these concepts had been nothing more than figments of speech until college.

And so I not only learned the game, I learned how to play it by playing with guys who were a lot better than I was. My roommate was from Staten Island, and he knew how to leave players flat-footed on the playground. A guy down the hall played on Derek Coleman's high school team. A friend I made at the gym played high school ball in Iowa, and nobody plays high school ball in Iowa unless he is good. I watched them play, I played with them, and they were attentive enough to realize that I really wanted to raise my game a few levels, so they helped me do it.

With very few exceptions, every player plays in games that are beyond his or her level, and will clearly be beyond his or her level until death. What keeps players happy is finding their level and being accepted into it. It confers the unspoken right to play with a loosely defined fraternity of people worldwide, and offers a reasonable challenge. The rules of pickup basketball, inside or outside, are that the winning team stays on the court to take on the next opponent. You play the game to earn the right to play the game. The privileges of acceptance include occasional invitations into games that are one or two levels higher than your accepted grade, but only as long as you can continue to be marginally effective. These are simple rules. They are not written down anywhere, nor are they ever enforced. If you play, you know them and you abide by them. The system works.

It just takes a little time to understand where you fit within the tiered echelons of basketball, much like it takes most of us a lifetime to figure out which of Dante's fiery tiers we might aspire to. Along the way, there are several important indicators that let you know you have earned the right to keep playing at any particular court or at any of the dozens of levels of the game. All of them are found in the subtle things that your opponents say to you.

In pickup basketball, you know you have earned your place in a special echelon when you are asked, "So, did you play?" This question doesn't refer to whether or not you may have played last night or last year, it is translated "what high school or college did you play for?" It is the ultimate compliment, especially for those of us who never played any organized basketball before being asked.

Another indicator that you have been elevated into the unwritten hierarchy of those who can play is when you truly challenge, or even beat, a better team, one in a higher echelon, and one who had a preordained right to take all comers at the court. This is not an individual accomplishment. It takes a polished group of players (quite distinct from a group of polished players) to win a basketball game against superior opponents. As trite as it may sound, a basketball team is truly as weak as its weakest player because an opposing team can and will exploit any weakness it can find every time down the court. This cliché is not necessarily true for all sports, but it is always true in basketball. I know this because there are games in which I have been that weakness. National League baseball games are not decided by which of the two pitchers is a better hitter. Three of the four players in a golfing foursome playing in a "closest ball" tournament could actually be dead or dismembered if the fourth player was a PGA pro. And, closer to my pedigree, a well-tuned brass instrument can drown out a poorly played clarinet with hardly any effort at all. This I know because I played the trombone in high school instead of playing basketball, and when the clarinets needed to be overthrown, I was there.

But in basketball, a weak player translates into some hysterical shot attempts at worst, and a free path to the basket at best, and these things matter. When a team wins a game, everybody on the floor deserves some of the credit. It was at the university gyms one late afternoon that some teammates and I tasted a piece of basketball nirvana as a team, and first earned our right to play at a higher level.

We had been playing half-court games for an hour. There were five of us left, an odd number—difficult to work with, and we were ready to get supper. Only a few other stragglers remained; everyone else was hungry too. Our collection of loose basketballs and gym bags was scattered across the far end of the court, opposite the doors. As we collected our belongings, the doors opened, five players walked in, and they started shooting around at the opposite end of the court. We could tell by their physiques, their shots, and their confident demeanor that they were good—clearly several levels above our humble echelon. We could tell by their inside jokes and camaraderie that they had played many games together as a team. They were fun to watch, but then we had to walk by them . . . almost through them as we left the gym—five of us through five of them. As we did, they asked us the chilling question we could feel even before it was voiced. "Wanna run?" A "run" is a game. To "run" is to play. The question is grammatically correct as either "Want to run?" or "Want a run?" When five players ask another five on a lonely court if they want to run, it is not actually a question. It is the unsheathing of an Elizabethan sword, a slap in the face with an eighteenth-century white glove, or gloves of more modern tailoring hitting the ice. It was a challenge that has only one reply. Supper could wait—we had a run.

Besides, this was a chance to test our skills at a higher echelon by invitation. By almost any standard, we were plainly the underdogs. They were fresh, we were tired. They were fast, we were slow. They were obviously synchronized, we were just five guys. They had muscle tone; we were engineering students. Perhaps our only advantage was that we were slightly taller on average, which is clearly important, but only for those who don't otherwise have the physique of strained linguine. Suffice it to say that with respect to altitude, we were on level ground with our opponents in every sense of the phrase. The only shame would come if we didn't make them break a sweat.

And so the game was on. One of my favorite college basketball color commentators has long been Bill Raftery. Like any notable sportscaster, he has a trademark, and his play-by-play partner always defers the first line of the telecast to Raftery, who emphatically announces the defensive set, but only with enthusiasm if the defenders begin the game playing man-to-man defense. Teams play man-to-man defense if their coach believes that the individual matchups are to the team's advantage. It is generally more demanding on the defenders, because each player is responsible for covering his offensive opponent over the entire floor. Playing a zone defense, defenders are sequestered in their "zones" around the basket, and are responsible for guarding against traffic through a specific spot. You are a private eye in a man-to-man set. You are a traffic cop in a zone. The trick with a zone defense is knowing when to leave your zone and assist on the strong side of the offense, where the majority of opponents happen to be. Bill Raftery respects the man-to-man defense. He seems to be somewhat less enthusiastic about the zone. As he opens his telecasts, his first words are usually something like "And here they go with . . . MMMMAN-TO-MAN!" If the opening defensive set is a zone, I think he gets up and takes a walk to get a hotdog or make a phone call. We would have been a big disappointment to Bill Raftery. There was no way that we were going to retain an ounce of dignity playing a man-to-man defense against this team—not a single matchup would have been in our favor. We opened up in a 3–2 zone, two at the top of the key and three along the baseline, hoping that our flailing noodle arms might be mildly intimidating. It was not very likely.

I have never played in a game with a pace as fast as this one. It was frenetic—we barely had time to organize ourselves into our zone defense before they were ripping through it with passes that were as quick and precise as laser eye surgery. Bill Raftery would have had a field day explaining our inadequacies. Even if we'd had our light sabers with us, we wouldn't have been able to see what we were swiping at. They played with energy, we played with urgency. Their eyes were wide with expectancy because they never missed their shots. Ours were wide with terror . . . because they never missed their shots.

I remember very few details about the game, except for the following two facts: it went on for a long time, and despite the comical mismatches on paper and on hardwood, we actually managed to stay close. It was almost a shame that there was nobody else at the gym watching the game. It would have been nice to play so well in front of a crowd of surprised peers, but more important, the game was longer because nobody was waiting for the court. The hallowed but unwritten protocol of pickup basketball clearly articulates that if there are players waiting to get on the court to play, games are played until one team scores eleven points (and each basket counts as one point in unsanctioned games). When nobody is waiting, games are played to fifteen or higher, at the mutual discretion of the combatants. In the shorthand of the hard-court, exchanged in brief grunts prior to each game, the ground rules are spelled out for all to hear. "Eleven by two, winners take," could mean a lot of things, but in just five words, the entire doctrine of the game is unmistakably enunciated (try explaining the scoring principles of baseball in five words or less: "Let's start with the balk . . . "). The game is played until one team scores eleven baskets, but the winning team must win by at least two points—a game with a score of 11–10 is not over, nor is a game that is 19–18. "Winners take" sounds fairly obvious—the winners usually do take the game. But here is where the pickup game diverges markedly from sanctioned games. "Winners take" means that the team that makes a basket retains possession of the ball and inbounds it for the very next possession. It works only for half-court games, of course. The only way the defensive team can gain possession of the ball is to rebound a missed shot, steal the ball, or hope that it goes out of bounds off of an offensive player. I always assumed that the rule was enacted to ensure that hopeless mismatches were ended swiftly, and there have been times I've been very thankful for it, from both sides of the score.

But this game was full-court, full contact, and "losers take," all of which are implied when five individuals ask another five if they "want to run." "Fifteen by two" was the only other necessary communication before the game started, and then it was on. And it went on and on. Had we played to eleven, we could have maybe caught our breath over the weekend. Although four more baskets don't sound like much, games played to fifteen are quite a bit more demanding than those played to eleven. For those of us who will never have the opportunity to play with an electronic scoreboard in front of paying spectators, playing to fifteen is fairly intense, on par with rediscovering all of your oddly named favorite childhood

Crayolas in your children's crayon box, like burnt umber. So we played to fifteen, without Bill Raftery.

> And whatever the reason, our zone or our shoes,
> We played toe to toe, unwilling to lose.
> The rim did not matter, their shots went clean through,
> But our shots went up, and they went in too.

> The defenses faltered, and absent that vex,
> The offense was stellar, much better than . . . well, it was good.
> Though clearly outmanned on both sides of the ball,
> We played til the scoreboard announced fifteen-all.

> It wasn't a real one, the scoreboard, I mean,
> But it said what it said, both teams scored fifteen.
> I'll say it once more, for it didn't seem true,
> But they'd scored fifteen, and we'd done it too.

> And what do the rules say in case of a tie?
> You keep right on playing, for victory's nigh,
> Or maybe it isn't, but what can you do?
> The rules clearly state that you must win by two!

Overtime. It is one of those jubilant expressions that roil the adrenalin, much like "fumble!" or "fight!" or "naked girl!" (I have fumbled several naked girls in my life). If you happen to hear the word, you stop whatever you are doing and take notice. Overtime. It is often the only fair and fitting way to end a game that has been masterfully contested by both opponents. In the final sixty seconds of the 1997 NCAA men's college basketball championship game between the Wildcats of Kentucky and the Wildcats of Arizona, both teams traded miraculous shots over and over, and both coaches let the teams play, even though they had timeouts to call if they'd wanted to use them. The game was to be decided without interrupting the frenetic intensity that had churned the arena from the outset, and when the buzzer sounded, everyone knew that this was the only way for the game to end. Overtime. Twice. The game was a spectacular display of players' talent and the coaches' inclinations to let them use it, and as entertaining as any basketball game I have seen since. The Wildcats won, and unless you were an alum, it didn't matter which ones they were.

Our game didn't have quite the national appeal as the Final Four, but to the ten players who paused for a moment at fifteen-all and looked around at one another a bit nervously, it had the same fervor. We were going to overtime. This had been unthinkable twenty minutes earlier, but here we were, nearly exhausted, and the run was going to continue. I think even Bill Raftery might have stopped to watch if he'd been there. Ball's in.

Not much else was said as the game progressed to its natural conclusion. One team was defending its honor while the other was gasping and clutching its sides in proverbial agony and ecstasy. It is nearly impossible to stay even with a superior team without finding that mystical Zen as a team known as "the zone" (quite distinct from the defensive setup). My team had found its Zen. We saw plays develop in front of us before they happened. We knew the outcome of a pivot or a sidestep before we moved our feet. We felt the ball slicing through the net before it rolled off our fingers. Our minds were just slightly ahead of reality, but not so far that our bodies couldn't hang on and follow through. These are the ways that confidence manifests itself in basketball, and in some ways they suggest that understanding the game in metaphysical terms is not as far-fetched as it may sound.

But Zen doth falter against conditioning. Two or three shots later and the game was over, just that fast. The overtime was as astonishingly quick as the rest of the game should have been, but our moment had yet to pass. Even in losing, as we doubled over to clutch our knees and desperately gather breath, the game once again transcended the small collegiate gymnasium, and we experienced that brief nirvana that comes with impossible achievements. The handshakes after the final basket were a long-lived trophy. When a vastly superior opponent looks you square in the eye, shakes your hand firmly, and says "Good run," you know that you have achieved a level of legitimacy that nobody can take away. They were trained, polished, disciplined, deliberate, and extremely skilled in the fundamentals of the game. They passed like lightning. They shot with precision and unbridled confidence. They defended their half of the court like wild animals on a fresh kill. They played with synchronized passion and motion. They were an NCAA Division I women's basketball team, and we had taken them to overtime.

My roommate and I played together in that game, as we did in so many games through our college years. We learned how the other played, where the other would be, when the other would break toward the basket. I learned a lot from him about how to play the game. It was he who hailed from Staten Island, where he had learned to play ball by the rules of the street. I hailed from a small, conservative Midwestern town and learned the fundamentals in my backyard. He was always a bit better than I was, and he usually won when we played head to head, but it was still a decent matchup. He was always at home on a basketball court, and had a moniker worthy of the game. Duke. He was 6'3" tall, I was 6'1" tall. Neither of us could dunk the basketball.

This last fact was an eternal truth that we would continually deny well into our late twenties, when we finally acknowledged the supremacy of the ten-foot rim. Not everybody can understand the angst associated with this unfortunate moment of self-realization, but throughout history, there have been some notable figures who know the madness of which I speak. Shakespeare's Macbeth was one of the most famous underachieving hoopsters, as evidenced by his famous soliloquy (reproduced with only nominal interpretive latitude):

> Is this a [nationally sanctioned rim] which I see before me,
> The [spring-loaded shock-absorbed steel] toward my hand?
> Come, let me clutch thee.
> I have thee not, and yet I see thee still.
> Art thou not, fatal vision, sensible
> To feeling as to sight? or art thou but
> A [nationally sanctioned rim] of the mind, a false creation,
> Proceeding from the heat-oppressed brain?

While the Greek, Russian, and Latin translations all use "dagger" and "handle" in my parentheses, most other linguists find it hard to contradict my interpretations. Most literary scholars don't realize this, but Macbeth was a highly recruited power forward coming out of high school. He was untouchable along the baseline, partly because he kept his dagger with him at all times, but he also surrounded himself with lots of talent. Hamlet won several MVP awards as a shooting guard, and King Lear held court every night in the low post. They once went on a fifty-six-game unbeaten streak until they played the Pirates of Penzance at King Arthur's fair. After that, the team slowly dissolved, thanks largely to grand jury indictments, suicides, incest, family disputes, and the institution of the salary cap. But their reign had been one for the ages. What remains unclear to scholars is whether Shakespeare was transferring his own inadequacies to his characters, or if he was simply portraying people whose extracurricular talents were limited to murder and lust, neither of which is a team sport, although. . . .

Clearly, the words above are those of a man who has heard the incessant harangue of a round steel rim ten feet above the ground. Yet history has chosen to focus more on the character flaws of Shakespeare's characters rather than on their athletic profiles and achievements . . . much like today's press corps.

A lot of players who are shorter than six-feet tall can dunk a basketball through a regulation rim. For anyone over six-feet tall and even mildly athletic, a dunk should be an attainable goal unless one's standards are particularly low. But for us, the mechanics of transferring speed into altitude never produced more than a few knuckles above the rim and some rough landings. It was Wesley Snipes, then an aspiring thespian, who, though not himself a Shakespearian authority, ultimately offered the most concise translation of the great bard's subtle yet timeless theme into modernity: "White men can't jump."

We faced this truth the way most vibrant and virulent young men do; we lowered our standards. The search for a lower rim wasn't as much a quest for self-improvement as it was a deep desire for hollow, yet eternally hollow, fulfillment. Hollow fulfillment isn't so bad, really. Wouldn't it be great if I could tell you that I once slept with a supermodel? It would, even though the whole truth is that I once slept in a hotel outside of Cleveland that brandished a sign reading "Welcome Victoria's Secret!" (They had left a few days earlier, but the sign lingered. You can't blame them). I would also like to tell you that I once advised our nation's leaders, even though the whole truth is that I sometimes offer opinions to public works directors. And, most certainly, I would love to tell you that I could dunk a basketball back in the day, even if the whole truth was that the rim was four inches too low. But even though we found a couple of rims in nearby playgrounds in Brookline and

Allston with rims that were obviously a few inches below the regulation ten-foot level, we still could not dunk. All we could manage was to ricochet balls off the back of the rim toward the stratosphere. Athletic prowess speaks for itself when some of life's most indelible memories include looking around to make sure nobody saw what you just tried to do.

But if dunking wasn't our game, we had the long shot, and a moment in front of thousands of cheering fans to prove it. I make this claim with only modest exaggeration. There were probably only fifteen hundred fans, but they were concertedly cheering for Duke and me. It so happened that we went to see our school's team play one evening, and through some incredible coincidence, both of us were randomly selected for the halftime three-point shooting contest. We were the only two who were selected that evening. The rules of the contest were slightly more complex than the rules of basketball itself. During the regular season, each of the randomly selected halftime laymen (two or three each game) was given six balls with which to shoot from beyond the three-point arc. At the end of the season, the shooters with the highest scores would participate in a shoot-off, and the winner would be awarded an all-expense paid trip to Florida for spring break—nothing to scoff at if you have a history of fumbling naked girls. The shoot-off was scheduled to occur during halftime of the conference championship game, barring any natural disaster, presidential overrides, or infectious diseases.

We strolled awkwardly out onto the court when our numbers were called. The aura was what you might feel if you walked into a court of law or the girls' locker room . . . "*I should not be here.*" I recall the feel of the court, the NCAA Division I–sanctioned court, hallowed ground. It felt like a firmament unto itself, and yet it was just a little springy. I immediately explained to myself that this was why the athletes were able to dunk a basketball, and why I was not. I was half-tempted to drive the lane and elevate when the attendant handed me my first ball, but I dutifully stayed behind the three-point arc, aimed, and shot my first shot. It went in. I put up the second shot. It went in. That's when I heard it, very faintly, as if only registering at a subconscious level. Athletes in big games with big crowds often tell reporters that their focus is so intense that they don't hear the crowd. I've heard pitchers talk about walking off the field after a phenomenal performance and not knowing if there were five thousand or fifty thousand people in the stands. I had always thought that these statements were pure bunk until I hit that second shot. I noticed the cheers for less than a moment before everything faded away except the rim and the backboard, but the distraction was enough. A purist would claim that even a split-second diversion is enough to spoil athletic rhythm, and the purist would be right. I took four more shots before I settled back into my groove, and then it was over. But as the sixth and final shot rattled around the rim and went through the net, I knew that the three shots out of six that I'd made were enough to put me in the shootout at the end of the season. Most contestants had made one shot, if that. I exhaled, stepped back from the line, and shook hands with Duke as he stepped in to take his shots.

I draw upon many classical literary allusions and parallels to describe my athletic endeavors to others: I would have thought that my three-point extravaganza would have inspired some obvious parallels to the Three Blind Mice, the Three Stooges, the Three Amigos, and my favorite, "Four men ride out and only three ride back," (the Eagles, 1973). But the legendary Monty Python troupe most clearly captures my moment of jubilation as the cleric famously instructs his slipshod band of warriors to launch their Holy Hand Grenade by pulling the pin, counting, and then throwing. He admonishes the band to count to three, and he emphasizes this requirement three times for clarity. To avoid ambiguity, he forbids the counting of any other number, citing by example three other ill-begotten numbers; two, four, and five. Three was his number, and so it was mine.

Duke followed with two or three of his own; I don't quite re-member. He made at least two, and if that was it, it was perhaps the only time I had ever outshot him. But that didn't matter. What mattered was that there were sports fans, real ones, cheering for us, and we both did well enough to be assured of a shot at the title soon enough.

The next morning I found myself riding the trolley up Common-wealth Avenue, when a familiar voice behind me said, "Nice shoot-ing last night." As this had never been a regular accolade in my world, it was followed by an awkward pause before I realized that the compliment was aimed at me. I turned to find the kid from Iowa with whom I had played from time to time, and who I had often tried to emulate. We came from the same mold, but he was poured from a higher-grade alloy with fewer voids and impurities. We were both 6'1" and about 180 pounds. To him, these features were an asset . . . to me, a gangly hindrance. Regardless, I thanked him for the compliment and we began talking about basketball. And that is when he asked it—the question that lifelong pickup players long to hear: "So, did you play?" It was an exalting moment even long after it had passed. "No, but thanks."

I practiced for weeks until I could hit about 50 percent of my three-point shots with some reasonable consistency. Our fan base understandably deteriorated over this period, and soon the Boston sports media stopped arriving early to catch practice. And perhaps that is how it was meant to be, a singular moment. If I had known beforehand that the conference playoff game at which the shootout was to be held would make national headlines for something other than the game itself, I would have been excited, maybe even giddy. But the headlines had nothing to do with us, as you can easily imagine. Although the NCAA had welcomed us onto its stage (as we like to see it), the Center for Disease Control just as quickly had us removed. For that matter, it had everybody else removed, too. Or maybe it was just the university avoiding litigation. In either case, it so happened that on the campus of Sienna College in upstate New York, the measles had recently broken out. I believe the campus was quarantined, but the Sienna basketball team was allowed out of the lockdown to travel to Boston for its big game. In Boston, the only people allowed in the arena were the players, coaches, and officials, all of whom were at risk of contracting the measles. No fans, no cheerleaders, no vendors, no bands, no halftime contestants. It was as if the two teams had met on the playground, and somebody said, "Wanna run?" There was purity in that game, which I watched on television, as there is in any game whose entertainment value is vastly outscored by its competitive spirit. I complained bitterly through halftime, knowing that I was missing an opportunity that had arisen purely by chance but that I had also worked for. But I think back now on the significance of that day for the players, who, rightly or wrongly, chose to play. I will almost certainly never again have an opportunity to earn a trip to Florida, or anything else, by shooting a basketball. But that deprivation pales against the unity of the players and the spirit of the game that day. Like Shakespeare and Python, Gilbert and Sullivan must have been basketball fans, too. Their Pirate King inquires with lilting affection,

> What, we ask, is life,
> Without a touch of poetry in it?

Clearly, he too was cheated out of a spring-break shoot-out.

So, we went back to dunk attempts to pass our lazy college afternoons—Duke and I, that is, not Gilbert and Sullivan (I bet they couldn't dunk either, and you can't set a pick in E-minor). And so it was that we found ourselves one day at a run-down court in nearby Allston, one with chains instead of nets, but chains that were hanging from rims that were just a couple of inches too low. Never mind that the neighborhood was unsavory, that there was rumored drug activity in the adjoining brick apartment complexes, or that the very mention of Gilbert and Sullivan would get you shot. The rims were low.

There usually wasn't anybody playing at these courts. The backboards were rusty, the pavement was uneven, and there were much nicer courts just a half-mile away (that also had one low rim). But somehow we were here this day, just Duke and I and nobody else, probably because we had a few friends who lived a few blocks down and we hoped they might have the same priorities we had on that afternoon. They didn't. But two other people did.

We had been shooting around for a while when we noticed two figures walking toward us from one of the apartment buildings. I would be breaking a Commandment if I told you that I did not feel conspicuously Caucasian. We were in a predominantly black neighborhood on a basketball court. How many millions of games have been played in similar venues throughout the country is a figure I could not even guess at. What I do know is that there have been enough games played in neighborhoods like this to endow the courts with urban mystique and imbibe the sport of asphalt basketball into the heritage of America's cities. The millions that have played, across the racial spectrum, have earned the right to call these hallowed lots their own. White, middle-class college boys with only marginal talent can learn a fragment of what it is to be a denigrated minority by stepping onto a court like this. Self-righteousness dissolves in a few heartbeats when you find yourself an obvious minority in a venue that accentuates differences, not in any derogatory sense, but just because of the antecedent human bonds. Four years of college taught us an awful lot about achievement, diligence, creativity, differential calculus, and other important introversions of the human soul. What we were about to experience in an afternoon would teach us an awful lot about its humanity.

The question was inevitable and really didn't even need to be asked. Two sets of guys walking toward each other on a lonely basketball court. When Duke University and North Carolina meet at center court, they don't pause to politely invite some friendly competition. Alexander Hamilton and Aaron Burr did not exchange good will before they exchanged lead slugs. Asphalt basketball is statistically not quite so lethal, but in the city it is not a sport for the gentle. "Wanna run" means "Let's get it on." I like to imagine that it is the very same phrase that medieval foot soldiers would exchange when meeting unexpectedly on the lonely Scottish Highlands. The only difference is that we had chosen not to wear our kilts that day. Damn good thing.

There was no hostility in the question, but it was not a Hallmark holiday greeting. As I've said before, basketball is not a sport laden with verbal encumbrances and ground rules. The game has in-bounds, out-of-bounds, and the hoops, all of which are plainly evident. If there is any ambiguity, that's too bad.

"Sure. We'll play." (A very suburban reply).

"Eleven, by two. Winners take." Nobody was waiting for the next game, but it was their court, their rules. We would play to eleven.

"Ball's in."

If you have ever played basketball at any level, you know that these two words transcend the day's events and take you from nonchalance or normalcy to very sudden self-awareness and focused intensity. Somebody who was not trying to vanquish you a few moments earlier now is. Time speeds up as passing lanes open and close that quickly, and time slows down as you notice and react to every subtle movement of the head, eyes, hands, hips, and feet of your opponent. The sound of your breath reverberates inside you, between your ears. Basketball is not a game that can be played casually. It is a particularly intense form of combat that is as cerebral as it is physical. You do everything at full speed and without hesitation, or you lose. You must see your lane or your shot before it develops, or it is too late. You must believe that your drop steps and pivots and fades and flashes will be successful, or they will fail miserably. Be ready. Be sure. Even when you are not.

But just prior to the intensity at the start of a pickup game, and frequently interrupting it thereafter if the game is played only in the half-court, is an odd ritual unique to the game of basketball. Customarily, the offense "checks" the ball to the defense, handing it over momentarily to ensure that everyone is ready. When the defense passes it back, "ball's in," and the game is on. It's a sportsmanlike gesture, really, and I make no real complaint about it. Nonetheless, Jack Nicklaus never tossed his ball to his paired partner to make sure the defense was ready. Roger Clemens never tossed the ball to a batter stepping up to the plate as a gesture of good will. And such generosity would be the death knell of the full-court game; "Havli-chek steals the ball! He stole it! Now he checks it with the de-fense . . . everyone is ready . . . ok, here we go!" Certainly, the luster would be lost. Granted, a check is not required following a turnover or defensive rebound, so even John Havlichek's great play would have been equally appealing in a two-on-two contest, though probably not as famous. You get the picture, though. Winners take, or "make it, take it," means that you retain possession if you make a shot. If a team has just scored, the defense was obviously not as prepared as it might have been, and checking the ball is simply tantamount to taunting without being rude about it—"Are you *sure* you're ready this time, chump, 'cuz I ain't comin' *at* you, I'm comin' *through* you . . . but only if you're ready, of course."

Not many sports can be played effectively after dividing the playing surface in half, and perhaps checking the ball is a necessary accompaniment to the division of the court. Golf can be played over nine holes instead of the full eighteen. Tennis in the half court would be hard to follow. Nascar racing on half of a track would be hard to survive, and the abrupt end might cut into advertising reve-nues. Baseball on half a field would be unspeakably mind-bog-gling. Whatever the sport, dividing the playing surface in half ne-cessitates some adjustments to the rules. Checking the ball prevents a runaway game in the half-court, but I've never much cared for it. The defense should be prepared to defend at any time without being asked. Be ready.

In much less time than it took to read or write that bit, the game was on. Bill Raftery would have been much more engaged in this contest than in the game against the women's team, because we opened up "Mmmmmman to man!" It's really all you can do in two-on-two. There are bigger holes in a two-man zone than there are in the ozone. We paired up with our opponents, who were no bigger or smaller than we were, and tried to hang with them. Both teams ran the standard two-man sets offensively; pick and roll, give and go, drive and foul. As with other games that have become personally monumental for one reason or another, I remember very few details, but I can recall with visceral clarity the palpitating intensity. The detail I do remember was that the game was played very close to the rim. We did not seize this game as an opportunity to avenge our three-point snub, however poetic that might have been. Duke and I knew how to get the ball to the net even if we couldn't elevate above it. People sometimes complimented us after a game by telling us that it was obvious that we played a lot together. It was true, we knew where the other would be and we knew how to set each other up. From the baseline or the perimeter, I would look to get Duke the ball as he drove straight down the lane—that was his shot. He would look to get me the ball on the baseline—that was my shot. Beyond that was improvisation. We never played with pizzazz, but when we were in synch, we were crisp and confident. When I wasn't playing with Duke, my game was much more peripheral. When Duke was on the court with me, we were storming the net (from below, of course). He elevated a part of *my* game that depended on *him*, and I cannot conceive of a more important hallmark of a good teammate. I only remember shooting once from the outside during this game, a turnaround jump shot from the left side of the key maybe eight to ten feet out. I do not recall if it went in.

Our game was on. We found the open man, we hit our shots, we pulled down rebounds. Our movement was controlled and laminar—no turbulence. Our adrenalin resonated with the unspoken meaning of this contest. I felt a dexterity quite unknown to me on most other days. But this was not most other days, and we were not in the gym back at school. We were on the playground in the city. Games in the gym are faster. Games outside are tougher. This was not a dirty game in any sense—it was clean and honest and sportsmanlike. But it was tough. You call a foul in games like this only if your livelihood is legitimately threatened. The guys we were playing against were good, and they were protecting their court. Our game was on, but we could not build any kind of a lead.

Among basketball's many quirks, one of its most intriguing is an old cliché. The New York Philharmonic does not go out of tune when boy bands play Madison Square Garden, and you cannot accelerate the line at the checkout counter just because the express line is moving faster. But unlike musicians and anxious shoppers, basketball players tend to play up or down to the level of their competition, as if the human mind and body are unwilling to exert themselves any more than absolutely necessary, but will do anything that *is* necessary, in their attempt to prevail. Our opponents were forcing us to put forth a monumental effort if we were to walk off their court with a victory, and in response, we played well above our usual plateau of competence. A coach would have been proud, but we had only ourselves, and there is no spare time during a game to feel proud. Then the game got really hard.

I have described how elite athletes can disengage themselves from their audience when they are intensely focused on a game. They neither hear nor see the spectators. It is, in my estimation, an enviable position to be so wholly yet ephemerally focused on just one thing, and I myself would strive for such Zen in my own job if ever there were a spectator. But I have experienced it, without trying, if only for those fleeting seconds between three-point shots, so I know that the pros are not making things up. I can also say

from experience that tuning out a hostile crowd requires consider-
ably more effort.

We were well into the game, perhaps not quite half way to
eleven, and both teams were matching each other point for point
and every drop of sweat. Whether the intensity on the court wafted
through the open windows in the adjacent brick facades, or whether
the customary time to assemble for afternoon hoops had come,
people began to drift out of the apartments to take up front-row
positions along the baseline and the one side of the court that was
lined with a small sparsely grassed yard. Evidently, they were all
well-acquainted with our opponents. Even more plainly apparent
was their fervent desire to see their friends win this game.

They did not come all at once, and my guess is that the two guys
we were playing against had simply arrived early for a game with
their friends, who were just now straggling down to the court. For a
short while, there were just a few onlookers, but before the score
got too much higher, there were at least a couple dozen. The game
was close, and the onlookers were having difficulty accepting that
fact.

"C'mon, man, you can't let *them* do that to you!" We were *them*.
That word can be fiercely intimidating not because of inference or
prejudice, but because of this country's inescapable history of racial hostility. It would have been intimidating if the neighborhood
had been white or Hispanic or Asian, but not as much so. Com-
pounding the intimidation, which was almost certainly devoid of
any malice, was the knowledge that so many marvelously gifted
black athletes have graced basketball courts at all levels, and the
fact that the game has become such a vibrant and iconic element of
urban life in so many predominantly black neighborhoods. America's black culture can legitimately lay claim to much of the evolu-

tion and character of this game. It is a hard claim to deny, and it should be a source of both ethnic and national pride. But the implications on this particular game were very clear; now it wasn't just their court at their doorstep in front of their friends, it was their game. "You can't let *them* do that to you."

A college basketball team draws alumni to its away games. Professional teams have fan bases in most of the cities they visit. We had nobody but ourselves and a decision to make. The score was close, probably seven to six or seven to seven. We had no way to gauge the true level of any hostility in the crowd that had gathered to watch the game, that is, to watch us lose. Nor did we have any idea how our opponents might react if we beat them in front of all their friends. The game had to continue—walking away would be tantamount to hurling epithets. The decision was whether to let the game finish, or to finish the game.

To this point, the game had been respectable by any standard— more so, perhaps, than many of the games in which we'd played back in the gym. There was no trash talk or even any harsh words from any of the players. It was simply a hard-fought game drawing out some passion from its spectators. Looking back, I believe that two truths, one quite personal and the other plainly evident to everybody at the court, helped me decide what to do. I had almost never stood up for myself as a kid on the playground, and memories of this childhood frailty linger to this day as a haunting shame. They ultimately evolved into an obsession to prove myself to my peers in my adult life, and I ceaselessly struggle between the extremes of too much vigor and not enough. But these memories are also gentle spurs in my side, of inestimable value. The second and more obvious truth was that in spite of any imagined or inferred threat or risk, this was simply a very good game that wasn't over yet.

And so the two teams continued to match each other point for point, to the growing dismay of the onlookers, and quite frankly, to our own chagrin. Until now, as the game had progressed and the onlookers had gathered, the experience had unfolded like a well-crafted symphony, or at least a nice sonata. Both teams were finely in tune. Plays resolved themselves like familiar chord progressions, in which outcomes can be anticipated long before they happen, but lose all their luster if the steps are not followed smoothly and pre-cisely. The crescendo of cheers and catcalls added a vibrant timbre to the acoustics of the game that otherwise would have been quite muted. Our opponents, their court, and their friends were the theme, Duke and I were the variations. Symphonies have four movements; Duke and I together had roughly four moves. The analogy is a stretch, but not a truly absurd one. Perhaps the only structural difference in this admittedly rosy metaphor was simply this: overtime. Our game went to overtime—the rules clearly state that you must win by two. As a general rule, symphonies don't do that. Sermons, perhaps, but not symphonies:

> You've just finished listening to Mahler's *Third Symphony*, con-ducted by a world class staff of coaches, assistant coaches, and trainers. As you can tell by the scoreboard, the strings and the woodwinds have yet to fully resolve the intonation in the fourth movement, and so this one is heading for extra measures. The combatants will meet at center stage for the coin toss, after which there will be one fifteen-minute sudden death period, followed, if necessary, by a shootout (in B-flat) and whatever injury time the official puts back on the clock. Let's see if the bassoons can regain their composure after the illegal formation

penalties and cramping in the third movement. Those really turned the tide against them.

Permit me a brief timeout to gather myself before we head to overtime. Every year when I watch the NCAA basketball tournament with the zeal of teenage girls following their pop idols, I keep track of the winners of each game and dutifully fill in the entries in my brackets as the tournament progresses, not so much to check my standings in the office pool as to identify and record the games or the series of games that were truly remarkable. It is an obsessive compulsion that I truly relish. And each year when I watch the tournament, I pull out my collection of completed brackets from years past and focus on the notes I've made in the margins and smile. Each year, with sixty-four teams competing, there is veritable certainty that some team or some player will do something unearthly, unbelievable in any other context. The very fact that any one team can win six games in a row against the best teams in the country seems entirely implausible, and yet it is an annual certainty. Other feats and statistical anomalies are less frequent, but at least one new one emerges every year. Let's take a little walk along the sideline:

In 1997, the University of Arizona defeated three number-one teams on its way to the championship. The Chicago Cubs might win a World Series before that happens again.

In 1998, the University of Kentucky (one of the number-one teams that lost to Arizona the previous year), recovered from point deficits of seventeen, ten, and twelve in its final three games before winning the championship.

The 1999 tournament was marked by the absence of the tournament's greatest allure. Not a single game was decided by a last-second shot.

In 2000, a year which saw two number-eight seeds reach the Final Four, Michigan State University won its semifinal game despite twelve scoreless minutes to end the first half, and they eventually went on to win the championship.

In 2001, Duke University recovered from a seemingly insurmountable deficit of twenty-two points in its semifinal game before ultimately winning the championship.

The year 2002 saw an uncommon rematch from the previous year. In 2001, Kent State University (a number-thirteen seed) staged a major upset of Indiana University (a number-four seed) in the first round. Opportunities for swift revenge are exceedingly rare in a tournament with so many pairings and permutations, but the very next year, the same two teams squared off again for a chance to play in the Final Four. Indiana exacted its revenge.

In 2003, the Gonzaga Bulldogs would have won their second-round game against Arizona if their last-second shot during regulation time had found its mark. They also would have won the game if their last-second shot in overtime had gone through the net. They also would have won the game if their last-second shot in the second overtime had been true. They lost the game.

In 2004, Georgia Tech won the preseason National Invitational Tournament, beating the University of Connecticut en route. The two teams faced each other again in the postseason championship game. Connecticut prevailed. This double matchup itself is extraordinarily implausible, but things didn't stop there. The very next night, the University of Connecticut women's basketball team won the national women's title. The Huskies will always be the first school to have worn both the men's and women's crowns at the same time, and geologic eras may come and go before it happens again.[1] This was a good year for New England. The Red Sox won the World Series in October after eighty-six years of trying.

In 2005, Sean May of North Carolina scored twenty-six points in the championship game victory over the University of Illinois. It was a good game, to be sure, but a routine box score. What made it extraordinary is that twenty-nine years earlier an Indiana Hoosier also scored exactly twenty-six points as Indiana won the championship game. The Hoosier was Scott May, Sean's father.

In 2006, George Mason University advanced to the Final Four. They won the eastern regional bracket to get there, seeded number *eleven* of sixteen teams.

In 2007, the Georgetown Hoyas defeated North Carolina to advance to the Final Four. The same two teams had met twenty-five years previously in a classic championship game, and North Carolina had prevailed. The 2007 game was billed as a marquee rematch, but what was astounding and peculiar was that John Thompson coached Patrick Ewing in both games, twenty-five years apart. John Thompson Jr. coached Patrick Ewing in 1982. John Thompson III coached Patrick Ewing Jr. in 2007. In 1982, the game was decided by one point. In 2007, it went to overtime. But even more improbable than the genealogy, depending on your level of statistical purity, was the fact that the two combatants in the 2007 championship game, the Florida Gators and The Ohio State Buckeyes, had also faced each other in the national football championship game just a few months earlier. There are 326 NCAA Division–I basketball teams in the United States, and 118 football teams of the

---

1. I was wrong. We only had to wait ten years. In 2014, the men's and women's NCAA basketball championship was again captured by the same school. Again, it was the University of Connecticut. In championship basketball games through 2014, the university is 13–0.

same caliber. Statistically, the chances that the same two schools that played in the football championship will meet again in the basketball finale are more than one hundred thousand to one. Even if the field were reduced to only those schools whose history casts them as legitimate contenders in both sports, it would be hard to improve on thousand-to-one odds. It happened, and Florida won both games.

The year 2008 was the first year in the history of the tournament in which all four number-one seeds reached the Final Four.

The year 2009 was the first time ever that all number-one, two, and three seeds survived the first two rounds.

In 2010, Butler University earned a five seed, and made it to the championship game, where they held the mighty empire of Duke to just sixty-one points. In 2011, Butler was an eight seed, and returned to the championship game (by defeating an eleven seed in the Final Four, Virginia Commonwealth University), where they held the powerful University of Connecticut to just fifty-three points. Butler lost both title games. Against Connecticut they shot just 19 percent and made only three two-point shots.

In 2012, Rick Pitino and his Louisville team faced Billy Donovan and his Florida Gators for a spot in the Final Four. Donovan had played for Pitino when he took Providence College to its improbable Final Four run. Pitino won this game, taking his third school into the Final Four.

In 2013, a number-fifteen seed, Florida Gulf Coast, produced two notable upsets to become the first of its seed to reach the Sweet Sixteen. They defeated mighty Georgetown, a number two seed, in the first round, and San Diego State, a seven seed, in the second. Also of note this year was a nine seed, Wichita State, which made the Final Four, then followed it up with an undefeated regular season in 2014, the only Division-I team in the country without a loss. They were invited to the tournament as a number one seed, only to lose to Kentucky, a number eight seed, in the second round. Kentucky went on to play in the title game.

Also in 2014, Traevon Jackson of the University of Wisconsin played against the five starting freshmen of Kentucky in the Final Four, and lost by one point. Twenty-two years earlier, his father, Jimmy Jackson, played for Ohio State against the five starting freshmen of Michigan (the "Fab-Five") for a berth in the Final Four. The game went to overtime and once again, the freshmen prevailed.

The trend is plainly evident and extends far back in time prior to my own personal historical records. But while all of these incredible feats are timeless and fascinating, the statistics that I record with the greatest zeal are the games that cannot be settled in the allotted forty minutes and require overtime. Unquestionably, the most exciting game I've ever watched was the championship game between Kentucky and Arizona in 1997, which went to double overtime after the final minute was played without timeouts and with both teams playing to a tie by trading spectacular shots. In fact, not only did Arizona win that game in overtime, that team also won its preceding game in the Final Four in overtime. Arizona had a good year in 1997. The 1995 tournament saw Old Dominion University, a number-fourteen seed, stretch its game into triple overtime before beating Villanova, a number-three seed. The East Coast stayed awake well past midnight watching that one. Villanova took its revenge against Boston College in 2006, coming back from sixteen points down to win the third round game in overtime. In 2005, three of the four games leading into the Final Four went to overtime before they were settled, the first time that has ever happened (the fourth saw the two teams separated by only one point with just one minute to play). One of the three games actually went to double overtime, and the others saw comebacks of fifteen and twenty points by the eventual overtime winners. Overtime roils the blood, even before it is even imminent. And so, we return to the pavement.

While our game that day was not recorded on anybody's brackets, it still went into overtime. This is its written record. Both teams had ten points, so the eleventh would not be enough to win. A twelfth point would be needed, but even that would be insufficient if the eleventh had first been matched. The game would continue until one team built a two-point lead. Win by two. Deuce. To the onlookers, this was like watching Rollie Massimino's eighth-seeded Villanova beat top-ranked Georgetown for the NCAA championship, or Jim Valvano's underrated Wolfpack beating "Phi Slamma Jamma" (University of Houston). It was the improbable bordering on offensive—all we needed was a coach with some Italian ancestry. The game continued.

I'm quite sure that nobody at the court that day remembers any of the details about the rest of the game other than this. It took at least fifteen or sixteen points to win. Overtime was not as quick as it had been when we'd played against the women's team back in the gym. Neither team wanted to relinquish its claim to the respect that would come from a victory, even if that respect would fade with the daylight, as memories of pickup games usually do.

"Point." In the tradition of pickup basketball and its verbal thrift, this word is another utterance marked by its brevity and unmistakable translation. It is only spoken when one team is within one point of winning the game, and it is usually spoken by the team on that verge, staccato and accented with bravado. It is a rallying cry for both teams to stand and deliver whatever they have left. If you don't, the next word you hear is "game." Game over.

"Point," echoed around the cracked asphalt court and its adjacent brick facades for a long time that day. I don't recall how many times we said it or how many times we heard it. "Game," of course, was spoken only once. We heard it.

It was actually a relief, to have lost, partly because we could walk off the court with dignity, and partly because we could walk off the court. The tension dissolved as soon as the ball sailed through the rusty rim. The handshakes were as genuine as they get, and both relief and respect were cast in the glances of all four players as we slowly uncoiled and regained our breath. And as breath returned, so too did the brief words that manifest the spirit of the game just as succinctly as other words capture its rules. "Good game." "Good game."

And for the moment, that was it, along with some jubilant proclamations from the onlookers, who had certainly become emotionally vested in the encounter. Our opponents drifted off to socialize with their friends, the onlookers, who were beginning to prepare for the next game. Having been defeated on a court with many players waiting to play, we knew our afternoon was over. We neither dallied nor dillied as we drifted off in the opposite direction to gather our belongings and head for home.

I will remember what happened next until the day I die, and hopefully longer. Having been born in the late 1960s after the great civil rights swell, and growing up with only the echoes of its anthems as a quiet backdrop to my personal Americana, I had experienced firsthand the hostility it sought to quell only once. As a twelve-year old boy, I spent a year with my family in a blue-collar town in the hills of central Pennsylvania, where my father was spending a sabbatical at a small liberal arts college. One of the boys who befriended me during my first week at my new school was black, one of only three or four black students in a large middle school, in a tough, predominantly white town. We became fast friends, Anthony and I, and I got to know him quite well during the year. I got to know him through his dread and his melancholy, and through the ways he met the oppressive malevolence of his class-mates. Most kids in the school threatened him repeatedly and boasted to each other about how they would beat him up if and when they got the chance. They justified their abuse on the grounds that Anthony talked too much and stuck his head in where it wasn't wanted. Their accounts were true—these tendencies were indeed troubling, but the truth is that they were Anthony's only defense against a small society that did not want him, for no other reason than that he was black. Anthony's face was uncommonly expres-sive. He smiled a lot, but it was an uneasy smile that never fully masked his alienation. He wanted nothing more than boyhood's normalcy, and I doubt that he ever found it. During the year that I knew him, there were a lot of days when his smile succumbed to an uneasy and unspoken question: "What do I do now?" This was my only direct exposure to racial hatred while I was growing up—it had never occurred to me that it could be so stifling. There was occasional tension in my high school between whites and Hispan-ics, but there was never any real hatred or ethnic abuse that I observed. Anthony was my window into the divide between blacks and whites, and the only palpable realization in my life that human nature might not yet be strong enough to acknowledge equality as a truth instead of an ideal. His was a lasting sorrow.

And the imprint of Anthony and his apprehensive relationship with the world was one of the reasons I felt so uneasy on the courts that day. However righteous our lenses on the world may be, the world is not monochromatic. The embers of racial oppression and fury may never fully cool, and they flare up with or without provocation from either direction. And so when I heard the call from behind us, my life paused. "Yo, cuz'—c'mon, stick around and run with us."

"Cuz." Cousin. In a tough neighborhood, after a tough game on his home court, in front of his friends who had almost witnessed his humiliation, a black guy was inviting two white guys to come play some more ball. He was surprised that we were leaving, and he called us back as cousins. Not brothers—that fraternity is sacred, and I understand that. Still, a cousin is kin, it's blood. At the time, Duke and I mused that nobody had ever paid us a higher compliment as athletes. I realize now that the words reached far beyond the bounds of the basketball court. Four guys playing ball on cracked asphalt on a hot day, united by a visceral passion for controlling a leather ball and for competing. His words were simpler than any civil rights anthem, but equally profound and resonant. Four guys with something in common. That was all that mattered. Al MacGuire, the late great basketball coach at Marquette University, used to counsel his players to take a year between college and their eventual careers and drive a taxi or tend a bar. That is how, he counseled, people can get to know and understand people. I think he probably also knew that you can learn a lot about a person by shooting hoops together.

I do not recall what it was that we had to attend to. A class, perhaps, or maybe an evening exam. More likely, though, we probably felt too much gravity. It wasn't just that our legs were listless, the situation itself had pressed an uncomfortable weight of uncertainty upon us. The fact that we bore no hostile sentiment toward our opponents did not mean that their racial outlook was equally tranquil. There had been no way of knowing, until now. And now we were exhausted. I have sometimes wondered how the second game might have transpired. It probably would have been a good game; five on five, full court. We probably would have teamed up with our opponents and could have run with them the moves they had run against us, and some of our own as well. We would have learned their names.

Chances are, too, though, that the second game could have diluted the first. That would have been unfortunate, for while we will never know if we were perched on the brink of another overtime thriller, we carried away a monumental memory of uncommon tension eclipsed by unequivocal civility. I sometimes wish we had stayed to play game two. I am often glad we did not. "Thanks, man, but we gotta go. Great game." It remains an ineffably great game to this day, cousin.

Almost twenty years later, I returned to that Allston neighborhood and tried to find the court, not to play, but just to see it once again. I could not remember exactly where it was, and so I circled the triangular blocks that delineate Boston neighborhoods for quite some time without any success. Later that week, the boundless pit of marginally useful information known as the Internet proved to be uncommonly useful and precise as I scanned online aerial photographs of the neighborhood and found the unmistakable image of the court squeezed between the thin strip of grass and the adjacent buildings. With the help of these photographs, I returned.

I turned off of Commonwealth Avenue and began to wend my way through the backstreets of Allston. As I got close, I noticed that the neighborhood was less neglected than I had remembered.

The two- and three-story apartments and duplexes were aged but not dilapidated. Still, it had born a sully reputation back in the day. Perhaps there had been some urban renewal in the intervening years.

I recognized the angular street that led away from a five-point intersection toward the court. I had been at this very intersection a few weeks earlier trying to find the court, but it had been dark, and I had taken the wrong street. In the daylight, the recognition was immediate—the worn down laundromat on the far corner, a few bedraggled brick-faced shops, and a long featureless industrial building, all leading directly to the court. I drove slowly, not wanting to be disappointed at memory's inevitable inaccuracies. And then I was there.

The backdrop was more or less how I remembered it—a windowless brick wall abutting one side of the court, the bland backside of a long and featureless apartment complex reminiscent of Soviet bloc tenements rising above the far end. A small grassy park, if it could be called a park, still lined one side of the court. The only difference in the surroundings was that a new eight-foot cedar plank fence now lined the far end of the court where a chainlink fence used to stand. It is literally a facade, an attempt to adorn an urban setting with suburban flavor. I preferred the old chain-link fence, with its bowed and sagging sections and ragged cut-through entryways. The cedar is nice, but it tries to segregate the old court from the old building, and truth be told, they work better together.

Apparently, the urban renewal will not end with the fence. The entire park was being refurbished when I visited, and was closed off from the sidewalk by a temporary chain-link fence. This was disappointing in more than one way—I had wanted to see the court the way it had been, to check the details in my memory with the aid of visual triggers. I had wanted to walk out onto the court again and look up at the basket that had been the focus of such intense concentration for a half hour on a hot day twenty years ago. But even that was gone. When I visited the court, the backboards and nets had been removed—all that stood at the ends of the court were the posts, two at each end. These two looked as if they had been planted into the ground quite recently and, they are probably just awaiting the coming spring to accept their new nets and backboards. I wonder if the nets will still be two inches too low. The frozen puddles that lay scattered across the court mildly assuaged the dismay I felt seeing a site that had once staged a monumental moment now being deconstructed and "improved." At least this meant that the asphalt was still uneven.

I don't make videos of important moments in life. My wedding was shot in still photography. We have hundreds of photographs of our children but very few videos. Videos often despoil life's most vital moments because they document the imperfections. Human memory captures the salience and grandeur of life's evocative moments almost perfectly, even if some of the details age with time. Memory draws from all sensory receptors, as well as the attendant emotions, and can, perhaps, wipe the dust off the polished antiques of the mind so that their grain and sheen show through once again. My memory of the game and the setting has not been altered by the new visual impact of the courts undergoing renovation. The game is as it was, and it will always be that way.

Nobody was there on the day I visited, just some heavy construction equipment parked off to the side. The court was empty, just as we'd found it before the game. But as I gazed through the chain links onto the court and tried to recall the gamut of emotions I experienced that long-ago day, my mind began to bring back the phantoms—first the players, then gradually, the onlookers. As I reconstructed a few plays while I stood there, and as I listened to the raspy sound of sneakers on hot asphalt, even the indistinct and jumbled voices of the onlookers came back from the recesses of memory for a brief moment. It was only then that I truly understood that in its mechanics, the game had been only a game, nothing more, just like any of thousands of games that have been played on that court; a bunch of guys doing what we did on lazy afternoons, some playing, others waiting for their chance to play, milling about and jawing with the players on the court. But because I remember the feel of the game, its instancy and its intensity, as well as its urban imagery, and because of its aftermath, it has always been one of the most transcendent moments of all my athletic endeavors. Yes, there are times I wish we had accepted the invitation to stay on the court and run in the next game. It is an uncommon gesture of respect to invite the losers of a game to play in the next one, even when there are already enough people for two full teams. But most of the time, I'm happy with the game as a singular memory of a time when doubt morphed into truth.

One might think that my basketball years were a spectacular failure if my most indelible memories are of losing two close games in overtime. My friends might mock me if they knew that one of those games was played against girls (if you've read this far, I need not explain the respect in this line). But by playing, my pals and I joined the legions of others who have competed well above their own level and have been invited back. That, to me, is the standard. We etched our names into *the game.*

"So, did you play?"

"Yeah, I played."

2

THANKSGIVING FOOTBALL

It is Thanksgiving Day as I sit down to begin writing this. The meal was finished hours ago, as was the revelry with friends and relatives. My own family is in bed, and I am the last to remain awake on this day of annual autumnal pause. Here are my thoughts.

Imagine a football stadium filled to its brim with one hundred thousand people. This is not American football, but rather, football that is ubiquitous throughout the rest of the sporting world—what we call soccer. Descend into its inviting symmetrical concavity, dissolve into its enormity, and find your seat. Feel the souls vibrate and reverberate off each other as their bodies chant and sway, rise and fall in unison. Absorb the pride of nationals as they celebrate one of life's most exhilarating (and least abundant) joys . . . a goal in a soccer game. Close your eyes and imagine this . . . and let part of yourself remain here amidst the expectant and jubilant throngs while we visit another venue, a cathedral of oak, maple, stately spruce, and an uneven lawn that is perpetually green and brown in equal measure. We are in my backyard, which, for one day a year, is a soccer stadium. For the past few years, Thanksgiving Day at our house has become known for *football*, not football. Not the whole day, really, just its twilight.

Several years ago, my wife befriended a single mother from a nearby city, a refugee from the despoiled East African country of Burundi. She has five children, ranging in age from three to seventeen years. They all came across the ocean, leaving behind a continent in which a home was a phantom ideal, not even a memory. Years passed in this country before she secured part-time work as a gardener, and in the meantime she stitched the days together on meager welfare benefits. Her English is broken, though she takes classes to help splice fragments together. This is how she met my wife, who had volunteered to help teach English on Tuesdays to anyone who might need to learn. Her outlook is no less hesitant than her voice on many days. Her husband is gone.

And so, for the past few years, she and her children have visited our home on Thanksgiving Day. After the meal has been served and the plates cleared, we shun the television and instead careen out to the backyard coliseum of trees, she and her children, I and my children, friends and their children. The late November sun has dropped beneath the brow of the trees and the chill is early winter, not late fall. But enough light remains, and though the weary afternoon air is frigid, we shed our jackets onto fence posts, one and all, and play soccer. Football. This is the sport that they grew up with, and from the moment the ball is put into play until we retrieve our jackets from the fence, their smiles betray a memory of a bygone life. Youth, by young and old alike, is reclaimed justly, and the joy on uncertain faces is so abundant that it moves me almost to tears. For you see, if we return to the football stadium filled with tens of pulsing thousands of people celebrating life and country, we must imagine them . . . gone. All of them. Stadium after stadium, completely wiped out, the souls in the seats nothing more than shadows and dust. This refugee mother of five children playing soccer in my backyard does not need to imagine. Her husband lies among the dead.

Football is the national sport of Burundi, but its profound joys have gone missing amidst the sound and fury of social upheaval (a sanitized term) that has beleaguered the small country for more than thirty years. The euphemistic unrest has been marked by violence and physical atrocities that could make humankind lose faith in itself should we dwell on the matter. And so Burundi is largely a forgotten country.

Our backyard Thanksgiving games would last forever if the earth stopped spinning to let the sun dangle by its own perpetual rays from the bare branches on the western hilltop. This bronze-grey twilight paints the spectacle of a woman shedding her native shawl and all of her cultural inhibitions so that she can better receive a direct pass from her teenage son and almost bicycle kick it into the small plastic goal at one end of the yard. This is the same woman whose sorrow weighs so heavy on her eyes and shoulders that she often sleeps in a corner of our living room while others gather, talk, and play. Stop reading this for a moment . . . put the pages down in your lap and close your eyes. Imagine it. Imagine this sepia-toned scene with your own family, your own mother receiving your pass and redirecting the ball in a single motion into the goal. Imagine her white smile as broad as oceans. Imagine. . . .

Until 1972, men of Tutsi descent, though a stark minority, controlled all military and state affairs of Burundi. They cemented governmental control when opposing Hutus rose up against them in that year. In response to the opposition, Tutsi leaders began a systematic campaign to suppress the one aspect of the Hutu population that posed a legitimate political threat—education. Rather, educat-ed Hutus. Education was the only avenue of advancement beyond the sterile fringes of peasantry for either ethnicity. Suppression of the most intellectually advanced would sap the remainder of the Hutus of any political locomotion and would establish durable con-trol for the Tutsi minority. To control means to dictate. To suppress means to kill.

And so the decision forced upon the Hutus was whether to fight or flee, and the stakes were mortal for body and spirit. By the tens of thousands, Burundians fled across nearby borders to Rwanda and Tanzania—reciprocity of sorts. After a social revolution in Rwanda in the 1960s, tens of thousands of its citizens had fled the country, some to Burundi. Two countries became alternating ha-vens for each other's brethren, if this word for shelter and sanctuary may be used so callously. But ethnic violence with militant inertia knows no boundaries or borders. Full stadiums of people were slaughtered throughout the region simply because they had once been born.

The twilight becomes dimmer beneath the vaulted arches of oak and maple, this democratic suburban sanctuary. Along the fringe of browned grass and boulders that delineate the field of play and separate it from the pillar trees, a mother and her child battle furi-ously over a loose ball. They laugh at their own intensity and at the beguiling angulation of the swales to nowhere that they must nego-tiate. From midfield, where I help guard casually against whatever may ensue or emerge from this contest at the verge, I wonder at the stakes in this game. I cannot comprehend what this family has lost—father, faith, home—but I can see what they are reclaiming in the dusk of November. Perhaps it is easiest to see without the full light of day—ivory smiles that affirm that the stakes today, at last, mean nothing at all.

After the Hutu uprising in 1972, when this mother was not even the size of the child with whom she competes for the wandering ball, her own parents fled Burundi into Rwanda and remained there. She remembers nothing of her own homeland. Through the 1970s and 1980s, as the Tutsi leaders solidified martial control of Burundi, political and economic instability, and terror, kept refugees beyond their own borders. There were attempts to civilize the government. A new constitution was introduced, but it never found traction. Who could think about games? What would they mean?

Then, in 1993, the country held its breath and its first free democratic elections. Intercontinental neighbors smiled and raised a glass at the rebirth of the nation. The celebration lasted for one hundred days . . . precisely the time it took for opposition militants to stage a military coup and assassinate the newly elected president, Melchior Ndadaye. Overnight, his democratic administration was supplanted by a military regime, familiar in its arms, new in its betrayal of hope. Intercontinental neighbors, for the most part, finished their drinks and then turned to talk to other guests at the party. Burundi was left alone again.

The Branch Davidians lost seventy-six lives that year in Waco, Texas. Some say the lives were lost at the hand of an overreaching government, others at their own hands—but at either hand, the earth paused. In East Africa, hundreds of thousands of lives had already been lost, and the hands bearing arms had overthrown any hope that this might stop. Hundreds of thousands more would perish. And the earth continued to spin.

But it can pause just long enough for the sun to linger in the western sky a little longer than it would on other days. These kids are fast. Even the younger ones can outpace me as I attempt to maneuver my Americanized body built for swinging bats and watching football on Monday nights. I quickly adopt a policy of shooting the ball immediately upon receipt. I have a chance that way. I cannot dribble with my feet through a crowd of on-rushers. I cannot complete an aerial kick or make a blind pass with my left foot. They can—each one of them, except perhaps the three-year-old daughter. The mother can do all of these things with the three-year old in her arms. This, friends . . . is a soccer mom.

This family's home country, an imaginary place to the children, was torn apart by the civil war that followed the 1993 coup. Retribution was administered by both sides, it found its resonance, and it amplified into hell. To most of the world, this was a schoolyard fight that would take its own course.

Finally, in 2000, ripples of international indifference swelled into waves of pressure, and agreements toward peace were forged. But the thirty-year genocide had swallowed stadium after stadium of thriving human beings, while mass sepulchers rose in their stead. As a common race, we can only hope that the spirits from within the slaughtered bodies retained enough breath to gather the names of the fallen and build cathedrals in our collective conscience.

Or, perhaps they are building many small chapels. The quiet sanctuary behind my house will fill itself to its brim once each year with players and on-looking trees. I have never asked this mother whether or not she wishes to return to her homeland. She was exiled from her country as a child, from her continent as a mother.

Instead of asking, on Thanksgiving Day we play football together. It is the national sport of Burundi, and by what I have witnessed, it may be no small measure of its soul. I hope that she and her children are thankful for this spirit that cannot be extinguished.

3

THE SEASON

We were not a perfect team. We had no perfect players. We did not have a perfect record. We never had a perfect game. Our season, though. . . .

The notion first crystallized at the moment when the ball reached the apex of its flight and started drifting down through the September sky, slowly passing through the lights that ringed the field, and down toward right field.

We played in the Cambridge Business League, an adult co-ed, slow-pitch softball league with teams sponsored by businesses in Cambridge, Massachusetts, just outside of Boston. Two years before, we had put up a record of eight wins and two losses before the wheels fell off in the first round of the single-elimination playoffs. This was the same season in which the Chicago Cubs and the Boston Red Sox, neither of whom had won the World Series in more than eighty-five years, had each been five defensive outs away from their respective pennants, each with a three run lead. They both blew it, and my heart broke twice that week. Ours was the kind of game in which the outfielders collide at full stride while trying to catch a ball. I was one of those outfielders. After the collision, the very next batter hit the ball to the exact same spot in the outfield, again splitting the distance between the centerfielder and me, and we both just watched it roll on past without moving an inch. It was that kind of a game.

In 2004, we only won three games and our subsequent shellacking in the first round of the playoffs was simply a formality. But that year was different. That year was the year that the Boston Red Sox won the World Series for the first time in eighty-six years. They won it just after midnight, under a lunar eclipse. Joe Buck's televised call on Fox Sports of Keith Foulke's midnight toss to Doug Mientkievitz for the final out has become as famous as Paul Revere's midnight ride—*"Back to Foulke. . . . Fans in Boston have waited a long time to hear it. . . . The Boston Red Sox Are World Champions!"* The words were polished and the delivery was very deliberate, and just like that, Boston changed. Printed words can do no justice to the impact of that moment. Grown men fell to their knees. Older men declared without hyperbole that they could die in peace. Drivers, Boston drivers, waved and smiled at each other for at least a week. And three million people came to town on the day of the celebration parade—that's just about one out of every one hundred people in the United States. Even a year later, when Red Sox second baseman Tony Graffanino committed a gaffe that likely cost the team a playoff game, he received a standing ovation the following day by a crowd that said unanimously, "Welcome back, Tony. Let's play another game." Boston may never be the same again. If only Longfellow had been a baseball fan, he might have foretold of Boston's second glorious midnight ride. It's not that much of a stretch, really. . . . The British regiments, the St. Louis Cardinals . . . they both wore red:

Listen, my children, and you shall hear,
Of a terrible curse that was vanquished last year.

In the late days of autumn in two thousand four,
Seen last by our great grandfathers of yore,
Some disheveled roustabouts stepped to the plate,
Swung their bats true, and ended the wait.

After Game Three, the Yankee's Grande Boss,
Put a hand to his ear to enjoy the fourth loss,
And to borrow a phrase that arises each year,
"That's a sound, grinned the Grinch, that I simply must hear!"

And he did hear a sound rising over the stands,
It started with anguished wringing of hands,
Then rose in a chorus of long-dormant joys,
The Red Sox had beaten the Empire Boys!

Then on to St. Louis, where foes overmatched,
Were quickly dismantled, throttled, dispatched,
A pennant, a trophy, which when last aloft
Most of the crust of the earth was still soft.

A man in the centerfield bleachers did perch,
Then rose and hastened toward Olde North Church,
One if by land and two if by sea?
Not this time, grinned he, this time there are three!

Yes, three lights aloft in the belfry did glow,
One for the conquest of each autumn foe,
Angels and Yankees and Cardinals all fell,
So rang he thrice the Church's great bell,

Then rode as a herald into the night,
Whose morning would christen the earth with new light,
Of splendor not witnessed in eighty-six years . . .
His message rang merry in New England's ears,

"The Yankees are conquered, the Cardinals are swept!"

He trumpeted, shouted, he laughed and he wept,
For every New England village and town,
The Red Sox had won baseball's coveted crown.

The following April, 'midst fanfare and tears,
Commoners, gentry, united in cheers,
New England proudly fell to its knees,
Unfurling its banners to April's new breeze.

Through providence, long-ball, and lunar eclipse,
The victory lingers on New England's lips,
A single word destined for hall-of-fame lore,
The curse that transfixed us shall be "nevermore."[1]

Hope springs eternal—success, a little less so. But it happens. Amidst the euphoria, the members of our softball team, many of whom had never won a championship in any sport at any level (that included myself), occasionally entertained the notion that if it could happen to the Red Sox . . . well, then, just maybe. . . .

The softball season that was ending as the ball arced through the September sky had begun just a few months after the Red Sox unfurled their championship banner at Fenway Park. It hadn't begun on the field that was now our stage for the moment. It had begun in a dimly lit lowbrow barroom just a few blocks away—the "midwinter meetings." A few of the guys from the team had gathered around a bar table, and when we realized that the highlights of

---

1. Several years after the Red Sox won the World Series in 2004, I was on a flight from Boston that made an unscheduled stop in St. Louis. I happened to notice that Theo Epstein, the general manager of the Boston Red Sox, was sitting up in the first class cabin. Startled by this fact and nudged by the coincidence that the flight was bounded by the two cities that battled for the exalted 2004 World Series, I silently slipped him a copy of this poem during the stopover, and walked away. At the end of the flight, as I exited the plane, I glanced down at his vacated seat. He had left some newspapers, a magazine, and several napkins strewn about . . . but he had apparently kept the poem.

the last season didn't even get us half way through the first round, we decided that the time for some changes had come. First, we agreed, we needed a new sponsor. We needed a new sponsor in the same way that a man needs a harem—it would be quite a coup, but tricky to pull off, and even harder to explain to everyone affected. Still, it was a remarkably good decision because our corporate sponsor of at least seven years at the time didn't even bother to call the team back together when spring came. Our season had been humiliating, but really . . . where would the Cubs be if their owner never invited last year's team back? (Okay, that's a bad example.) But, there we were without a sponsor, so we got one. Overnight our identity changed from that of a locally popular firm with an environmental motif to that of a national record store franchise with in-your-face branding. Now we had some chutzpah. Green is good, and none of us had anything against our former sponsor or what it stood for, but its logo was a green Volkswagen Beetle. It is exceedingly difficult to knock the leather off the ball when you have an artsy little sketch of a Volkswagen Beetle on your jersey, and you almost feel the need to apologize when and if you actually do. Our new sponsor doled out shirts with pictures of Adam Sandler's head plastered on the front and his repertoire of R-rated comedy routines splattered on the back. Although they didn't arrive until late in the season, the prospect alone brought the swagger back.

But there was still the matter of a lineup. Swagger is great for morale, but it needs to be convincing for it to have any effect on the outcome of a game. We realized that not everyone on the team wanted to swagger. There's nothing wrong with that. These were first-rate people, the kind you would want to read your eulogy and who would undoubtedly make sure you looked comfortable in your coffin once your time had come and gone, but in competitive softball, merit doesn't come with fondness and good cheer. It comes with batting average, golden gloves, and a strut. We didn't quite invite them back to camp in the spring, and truthfully, we still feel bad about it. But the truth is, too, that our sponsor didn't invite any of us back. In the end, I think there is a little bit of George Steinbrenner in all of us.

And so we rebuilt the team. Half the lineup, those of us sitting around the bar table that night and a few others, remained unchanged. The problem is that those of us sitting around the bar table that night, with perhaps one or two exceptions, couldn't run the forty-yard dash in anything less than 12.3 seconds, and even then we had to do it as a relay. It's not that we were overweight and playing in a beer league, we had just had enough orthopedic surgeries among us to be offered an endowed chair at Harvard Medical School. But true to our sport, we declined the chair and settled for a comfortable seat at the bar. And that is precisely where we determined that we needed some speed.

So we got it. We picked up a few guys who could circle the bases in the time it took most of us to drop the bat and take our glucosamine. We also needed some women. Not at the bar, on the team, although I suppose. . . . Now, I must admit that I was sharply rebuked by a female friend when I mused about our situation to her and blurted out my sentiment that "life is one continuous search for good women." She actually never really spoke to me again without a deeply suspect tone, the kind that most wives master in the first month of marriage. Poorly chosen words, perhaps, but none are more apt to a softball team trying to rebuild itself in a reasonably competitive co-ed market. We needed some women.

So we got some. Not "got some" as in "I got me some!" but as in "we acquired some female talent." No, that doesn't quite work either. We found some women who knew how to score. Hmmm, nope. It seems that these days, it has become impossible to say that we recruited some women with extraordinary talent on the diamond without making it sound like we dragged them into the back room for all sorts of unsavory rituals. Suffice it to say that these girls could really swing. Aw, hell. Last try—each one played with a remarkable mix of grace, intensity, and congeniality that truly knit the team together. There.

And that was our team: the fleet, the beat, and the sweet. Most preseason polls placed us somewhere in the middle of the pack of nine teams, and we ourselves figured that it was a rebuilding year. We hoped to have a record of 0.500, splitting the difference between our last two seasons. We lost our first game but rebounded quickly and won the second. Our goal was looking pretty good.

Then things took an odd twist for me. By "things," I mean my leg, and by "odd twist," I mean exactly that. During the pregame warm-ups before our third game, I managed to pull my thigh muscle while stretching and playing catch. This was the second time I had fallen victim to the same beguiling evil—in college I sprained an ankle so badly playing pregame catch that I was on crutches for a week. I've long acknowledged that I was pieced together with leftover parts from the bottom rack, probably to meet an end-of-month production quota. This was simply ridiculous, though. Were it not for the fact that quirky injuries happen to other people, I would demand to see the warranty papers that came with my arrival at birth. I am mildly assuaged by the anecdote of a friend who one spring walked out onto his favorite golf course for his first round of the year, teed up on the first hole, drew his driver back, swung, and broke his leg. In my case, I was so humiliated that I'd disabled myself while playing catch that I trotted out into the field with the rest of the team when the game started. Well, they trotted. I moved as gracefully as a drunken camel. My swagger had morphed into a stagger.

I planted myself in right field and told myself that I wouldn't move until the inning was over. Not many balls get hit to right field, and so my plan seemed reasonable enough. Alas, naturally, on this night a high pop-fly sailed over the first baseman's head and right toward me, on a trajectory that would drop it about twenty feet in front of where I stood balancing on one leg. A routine fly— on any other night, it would have been automatic to slowly drift under the ball and make a casual catch. But on this night I couldn't run. The only way that my working muscles could translate the signals from my brain and propel me forward was if I flopped toward the ball like a fish trying to scramble back into the water. I used to wonder what Lewis Carroll was thinking as he wrote the first line of his poem about the Jabberwocky, but after this play, my wondering ceased:

> Twas brillig, and the slithy toves
> Did gyre and gimble in the wabe.

The only question was whether I was a slithy tove or the jabber-wocky itself. I certainly gyred and gimbled, apparently in earnest because my hat flew off and it was decidedly not due to my ground speed. All of this notwithstanding, I actually caught the ball. Lewis Carroll saw me coming, because his famous poem continues:

> He left it dead, and with its head
> He went galumphing back.

I galumphed right over to the bench, and eventually played catcher for a few innings later in the game. I told a few of the guys the next day that I was probably done for the season because pulled muscles can take a long time to heal. But two things drew me back. It was this third game that saw one of our finest team performances, a 13–0 shutout of a team that usually beat us pretty handily.

> All mimsy were the borogoves,
> And the mome raths outgrabe.

It wasn't all us. Our opponents that night had a mimsy game indeed, but we outgrabe them every inning. We made plays worthy of some airtime on SportsCenter that night. First, the entire lineup, top to bottom, hit with conviction and consistency. This team of ours, I began to see, was the real deal. Second, I really didn't want to be remembered for my crippled flounder routine in right field—I hoped to have a chance to make a slightly more graceful play out there.

And besides, the next game was against our nemesis, a group of players renowned throughout the league for their asperity, for using bats that had just a little more than the allowable pop, and for picking fights with whomever happened to be in their way as they rounded the bases. They were good, no question, but they were beatable and we knew it. We had just never managed to beat them. Two years earlier they had throttled us and had tried to pick a fight in the process. Last year they had thrashed us so soundly three games in a row to close out the season that we were ready to take them up on their next offer for a fracas just to save some face. They had pounded us in our final regular season game, they had performed an encore the following week during a makeup game of an earlier rainout, and then they had knocked us out of the playoffs in about an inning and a half.

One of the twentieth century's most inspirational philosophers and philanthropists once broke character and quipped that everybody, animate or inanimate, needs a nemesis. She was right. A nemesis is an odd thing, really. It is distinctly different from an archrival, who plainly acknowledges the mutuality of bitterness and bad blood. Most nemeses don't even know that they are nemeses; they just continually flummox, thwart, and pester their adversary without fully appreciating the psychological obsessions they are creating. You beat an archrival to make the crowd scream and cheer. You beat a nemesis to conquer an inner demon and get on with life. The rules of engagement allow you to buy your archrival a round of drinks, but any kind of social entanglement with a nemesis is strictly forbidden. They are to be kept mysteriously distant and are to reappear sporadically throughout life to offer fleeting opportunities for the oppressed to stand and deliver. Those who are not primed and ready for these chances will be blindsided every time. Life with a nemesis has more romance, more crescendos, more vital ebb. I wasn't going to miss this game because of a muscle I pulled while playing catch! This arrogant and invincible team was in our heads, and it was time to *vince* them.

I should have waited. There was to be no reprise of the "Miracle on Ice" that night. Perhaps if we had worn ice skates we might have kept it close. Reminiscent of my dates in high school, I, myself, committed the first and most crucial gaffe of the evening. It was the kind of blockheaded play that any major league fan would lament long after the merciful offseason trade of the offender for a minor league equipment manager. Any good nemesis will tell you that their primary tactic is simply to wait for their opponents to defeat themselves in their moment of opportunity. Our moment came early in the game when we were trailing by several runs but had the bases loaded with just one out. My leg was still stiff, but I'd managed to hobble to third base on a string of base hits, and there I stood. Rather, there I *should* have stood. The next batter hit a line drive down the third base line and without thinking, I vaulted myself from the bag toward home plate with all the fury and dexterity of a rabid chicken, not because I had to beat the ball to the plate, but because the runner on second base was sure to overtake me if I didn't get out of the blocks in a hurry. I took three or four steps and then heard the sound that followed the fury . . . leather on leather, ball meeting glove. My gut wrenched, and I skidded to a stop and tried to flop back to the base, but the third baseman had already casually stepped on the bag after making the catch. Double play. End of inning. Three runners stranded in a close game against our nemesis. "Oops" was not the word I chose to express my feelings to those present. It was never close after that. Our wheels fell off and we lost 9–2.

The watering hole where we either drowned our sorrows or raised our glasses after our games was even lower-brow than the bar in which we'd hatched the plan for this team. But our performance this night was not even worthy of a twelve-dollar bucket of Pabst, so we disbanded and went home. Normally, we revel in the fact that we can buy dinner for four for $8.95 and keep the cardboard. We became enchanted with the notion that the beer cost less than the ice that keeps it cold. The real charm of the place was its people, as can probably be said of any bar that attracts local regulars every night. We never quite figured out who these people were or from what walk of life they came and went. Almost all of them appeared to be down on their luck—mome raths and borogoves if ever there were such beings. Almost all displayed distinct and jarring grooming above their collars that suggested that they had either resigned themselves to their fate or were trying too hard to overcome it. But in this place they had found companionship, a place to talk even if nobody but the beer was listening, and a very basic kinship. I am sure that our presence turned the somber but comfortable mood into something a bit more restless, and although occasionally one of the inebriated locals would attempt to strike up a conversation with us, we were never really welcome. We perturbed what was probably the singular point of refuge for these people. On the night of our demoralizing loss, it was better that we didn't add to the gloom.

Mercifully, we had the next week off so that our souls could go through rehab. We returned to the field the following week on a hot July evening, rather perfect for a ball game. Our record was right at 0.500, right where we had imagined it should be. But we were better than a 0.500 team, and we knew it. We'd watched each other play and we knew that we could play with the best in our league, we just never seemed to be able to do it. On this night, we wouldn't have to. Our opponents offered about as much resistance as a dead fish.

The crowd at this game was larger than usual—almost double digits. And despite all of the things that happened on the field that night, it was the convergence of three fans in particular and some uncommon luck that turned an ordinary summer evening at the ball field into something extraordinary, for me at least. My family was visiting for a week, and my father decided to come and watch the game. He had taught me how to play baseball when I was five years old, and had watched me play as a kid, but hadn't seen me play a game for twenty-five years because I hadn't played very many and because we live in different states now. Every time I stepped to the plate on this night I felt the five-year-old inside me saying, "Watch this, Dad." I also brought my three-year-old son to the game on this night. I had taken Ben to a game at Fenway Park when he was two years old. He enjoyed the game for about three innings, and then turned to me and said quietly, "Daddy, let's go home and find

Mommy now." This night, though, was the first time he would ever see me play in a game, and he was willing to stay for more than just three innings, even if he spent most of his time playing with his Grandpa and our pitcher's son behind the bleachers.

But that was not all. I mentioned that there were three fans in the unusual convergence of good fortune on this night. Woodward and Bernstein would just be two guys had it not been for Deep Throat. Larry and Curly would still be spinning in circles had it not been for Moe. The big bad wolf would be driving up the price of pork worldwide had it not been for the third pig. One of my good friends on the team (not Curly) invited his girlfriend to come and watch this night. It was the first game she had attended, and while she didn't offer mysterious evidence about conspiracy theories or pound anyone over the head with a mallet, she did bring a professional-grade camera. She spent the evening taking pictures of the team—action shots and unguarded moments. Her timing was so exquisite that I later used one of the pictures to deconstruct my swing and discover that my balance was all wrong. She also captured people smiling in their most natural moments, and whether it was skill or simple grace, it was unquestionable artistry. She developed the pictures in black and white, displacing the game in time and gracefully separating it from all other cares. Among the many photographs that adorn the shelves and pages and shoeboxes in my home, I now have one that is truly priceless; my father, my son, and me, standing together on a night in July at a ball game, in black and white. My father is wearing his Cubs hat, the same one he probably wore to all of the games we watched together at Wrigley Field when I was a kid. Whatever the outcome of the game or the season, I had my trophy.

We won that game 34–3 in four innings. As for the season, well, that is the rest of the story.

If our offense was inconsistent, our defense was anything but. The next week, on an evening with air so thick that home runs gave up and became routine flies, we scored a meager three runs. The other team didn't score any. We lost the next game when the umpire called the game before it was over. I'm not sure what was on television that night, but I guess it was better than our game.

So, we walked onto the field on the last night of the regular season one game above 0.500. Whatever the outcome, we would have achieved our unspoken goal for the season by having lost no more games than we had won. But by now we had learned that our team was potent, that we could trust anybody in the lineup to deliver a clutch hit or to take base hits away from the other team. We wanted to win our final game and complete the season with a winning record, and so we did. We came from behind twice that evening, once in the last inning, and walked off the field with a winning record. At five wins and three losses, it was not a stellar record, but it carried us into the playoffs with a number-four seed. The number-one team was undefeated. The number-two team was our nemesis. If things stacked up the right way, we could end up playing both of them. There is nothing quite like baseball in the twilight of the summer.

You would be hard pressed to find a slow-pitch softball game that can truly be classified as intense, but at any sport and at any level, single-elimination playoffs kindle the adrenalin. The experience and the aura, if not the screenplay, are profoundly accentuated to the players, even if the magnitude of the event is lost on the fans, or more precisely, the passersby. When you step to the plate during a regular season game, you might think to yourself, "That chili dog

I had for lunch was a bad idea," or "spandex really doesn't work on their second-baseman," or you may recall Homer Simpson's sage advice, "You tried and you failed. The lesson is, never try." Step to the plate in a playoff game, and your mind leaps several orders of intellectual magnitude. You hear the hallowed words of Jim Valvano, Vince Lombardi, and American presidents; "Don't give up. . . . Don't ever give up." "Winning isn't everything, it's the only thing." "Four score and seven years ago. . . ." "I did not have sex with that woman." You hear the "Battle Hymn of the Republic," starting faintly in the distance and building in a crescendo to a thousand voices. And amidst these more eloquent admonishments, you hear your own soul speaking quite firmly . . . "Don't f*** up."

Game one in the playoffs pitted us against our friendly rivals, the jocular team that had walked off the field with our pride two playoff years ago, but whom we had shut out earlier this season in one of our finest ever team performances. They were classy and they were good, and there was never too much shame in losing to them, no matter what coach Lombardi told us before the game. This year, betting on either team would have been foolish.

Our comeback victory in the last regular season game had us brimming with confidence . . . so much confidence that before the second inning was over, we were trailing 6–0. As we glumly strolled into the field in the third inning, the center fielder called over to me, "Hey, I stole out of work tonight so I could make it to this game, and I didn't do it so we could lose like this!" I thought about this for a moment. It sure seemed as if we were going to lose. Our slouches and shuffles announced that we were ready to give up. We were ready to succumb to a toned-down proverb that winning isn't everything; it's the flowers and rainbows along the way. We hadn't been able to four-score, and there were certainly no women waiting to have sex with us even if we could deny it later. It took me awhile to get past this last thought, but when I did, I remembered that we had what was probably the most dependable top to bottom batting order in the league, one that could start firing at any minute. Guy or girl, old or young . . . less old, fleet or beat, we had one thing in common: we could put the ball where they weren't when we needed to. I called back to the center fielder just a few short words before the inning began. "Don't worry, we got this." And as I said it, I think I believed it.

And we actually did four-score in the next inning while keeping our foe scoreless. An inning later we scored three more runs and were ahead 7–6. Nobody remembers any of the details other than that we manufactured runs and chipped slowly into the lead until it was ours. After that came the glamor. Our first baseman made one of the finest reflexive plays I've ever seen on a softball diamond, diving to stop a screaming line drive down the line that would have allowed the batter to circle the bases three or four times if he'd wanted to. You could feel the other team deflate. Late in the game, with bases loaded and two outs, one of our most powerful hitters laced one over the center fielder's head to drive in three runs and put the game out of reach. Before the game was even over, our opponents were congratulating us on a great season and a great game. And with unfailing class, after the final outs were recorded and the traditional line of handshakes was complete, their captain walked over to me and handed me his phone number. "Call me," he said, "when you find out when your next game will be. We want to come and cheer you guys on." Games and seasons come and go, but acts of supreme sportsmanship are lasting. Amidst the clutch hits and great defense that etched our season, this was one of the most unforgettable highlights, accented by the fact that they actually did it.

With that win, we found ourselves in the semifinals, set to square off against the undefeated number-one team. At this point, we figured that we had had a good run, that anything else would be gravy. But we silently pondered this: Would Jim Valvano's famous speech have been so inspirational if his dictum hadn't been so absolute? "Don't give up unless you know you are about to lose. Accept that you are a loser, and anything else is gravy. Isn't that great?" Or would Vince Lombardi, Valvano's idol as a coach and the man he quoted in his famous speech, have lit the fire he did if he'd admonished his men, "Gentlemen, we will be successful this year if you can focus on three things, and three things only: Your family, your religion, and *gravy*." And Bill Clinton's infamous rendezvous would have been a page-three postscript if he had simply declared, "I do *not* have sex using gravy." Perhaps what makes great words great is that even though they can be neither proven nor disproven; they are simply the truth (with the notable exception of sworn presidential testimony). We knew the truth, and that truth was that we should not give up.

I like to think that one of my good friends is Mike Krzyzewski (aka "Coach K"), head basketball coach at Duke University. Well, more precisely, I once injured my shoulder severely and was evaluated by a half dozen doctors, one of whom had worked for a while as the team surgeon for the Duke basketball team, and therefore had probably spoken with Coach K once or twice. I didn't actually see or talk with this doctor, but was told that he had screened my x-rays and advised me never to play basketball again. So the connection to Coach K was there, you see. Anyway, however tenuous my relationship with the front man at Duke may be, I do admire the lessons he instills in his players. In his book, *Leading with the Heart*, he counsels, "Be one of the teams who believes you can win it all. But don't assume that you *will* win it all." As the days passed and the semifinal game drew nearer, I think that every member of our team began to believe that we could defeat the number-one team. But we also knew it was going to take a nearly flawless game.

You could read confidence on the faces of the players as we assembled in the third base dugout on the evening of the game and started tossing balls along the left-field foul line to loosen up the muscles. Everyone was smiling, relaxed, and proud. If there was any lingering doubt about our team's resilience, it wasn't because of our performance. It may simply have been the fact that we hadn't latched on to any kind of iconic identity. Although arguably the intellectual equivalent of frat house existentialism, having a mascot is a powerful way to unite human souls. I might probe into the reasons behind this, but I admit some trepidation. I am afraid of what I might discover. Why would we strive to make a goat with a cape proud of us? Suffice it to say that a mascot is a blameless and acceptable form of expression for those thoughts and noises and gestures that might otherwise go unoffered, and a rallying point for the intangible energy that arrives with players and fans to big games. On the night of our semifinal game, our mascot arrived, and we didn't even know he was coming.

As promised at the start of the season, our sponsor finally brought our team shirts, leftover from a recent comedy tour that had passed through Boston. On the front was the mug of comedian Adam Sandler, smiling his incorrigible smile. On the back were the names of the comedy routines that comprised his recent tour. These were not for children, and they were enough to make the other team look twice to ask, "Do their shirts really say *that?*" We are not raunchy or disrespectful people; we just found our chutzpah in a cheap cotton blend. The piece de resistance of the ensemble was emblazoned on the left sleeve of each shirt. Apparently, one of Adam Sandler's comic sketches features a robot that happens to be gay. This little tin man adorned the sleeves of our shirts, proudly wearing a tight white tank top that unabashedly revealed every nut and bolt. As we stripped off the t-shirts we'd worn that night and proudly replaced them with our new "uniforms," we knew we finally had a mascot as well. All of our energy was now channeled through a homosexual automaton, and you would have had to look hither and yon to find more unity on one team.

And yet the enthusiasm that had washed through the dugout before the game waned almost as soon as we took the field. As if rewinding to our previous game, within two innings, we were trailing 5–0. Neither I nor anyone else on the team remembers how the other team scored their runs, but what we do remember is that something changed again, and I would be dishonest if I didn't give just a little credit to the happy little fellow on our sleeves. Let's be honest. If, over a span of two innings, you can come to terms with the fact that you are brandishing a gay robot to the world, then self-confidence and hypertension are not likely to be high on the list of your life's problems. We got what good teams get at some point in a big game if they expect to win it, and attentive spectators and commentators can usually pinpoint the exact moment at which it happens. We got loose. And as much as anything else, it was this ridiculous notion of trying to look good for a make-believe mechanical spirit that helped us forget where we were and who we were playing and to simply play the way we could. I said it before—a mascot is a powerful way to unite human souls. We started hitting in streaks and scoring runs. In our minds, this little tin man on our sleeves had become a giant fifty-foot inflatable mascot suspended over our field of dreams, smiling down upon our every at bat.

It was not a quick or easy comeback. We scratched and clawed our way back all evening until we sat poised to bat in the top of the seventh and final inning. We couldn't quite believe our situation. After the bleeding in the first two innings, we had held this heretofore undefeated team to just one more run in the next four innings, and had managed to score runs in bits and pieces ourselves. All year long we had relied on simple error-free defense and stringing singles and walks and occasional extra base hits together . . . blue-collar baseball if ever it was played. As soon as we had remembered that we could do it, we did. With one inning to play in the semifinal game, we had a 7–6 lead.

If we were surprised, so were our opponents. As we looked out from the dugout into the faces around the infield we could see that they were not accustomed to finding themselves behind this late in a game. Other than our own faces and those of our hopeful fans, there was concern and unease etched into every other face . . . except for one. One face was remarkably happy, almost giddy. It was the face of the captain of our nemesis team, who had already won their semifinal game and were preparing for the championship game the following night against the winner of our game. He had come, alone, to scout both teams, and with unbridled enthusiasm, root for us. A win by our team on this night, he must have figured, was a virtual lock on the championship for his team. So he sat in the stands and kept notes on every batter and made no friends anywhere by yelling at our fielders to position themselves where our opponents were "statistically" most likely to put the ball into play. We paid no attention—our defense was sound at every position and statistics simply don't work that way or any other way in slow pitch softball. It aggravated our opponents, though, for good reason. They knew who he was and why he was trying to help us instead of them. They tossed a few utterances in his direction during the game, but in the end, we all just ignored him and let him make a fool of himself. The gay robot just smiled.

I was one of the first to bat in the top of the seventh and final inning. We all knew that a one-run lead was unlikely to hold up, and I was not nearly as loose as I had been earlier in the game. Usually, when I step to the plate, I scan the field for a gap, then wait for a pitch that lets me angle the bat to drive the ball toward that gap, wherever it may be. In clutch situations, though, I try not to overthink things like this—I just wait for a good pitch and try to make good contact. I know my history and I know that statistically there is a better than even chance that I will get a hit this way. But as I looked out into the field this time, I couldn't help but notice that the second baseman was shading way over toward first base, leaving an enormous hole right up the middle. I decided it was too good to pass up, and I waited for a pitch right over the middle of the plate, about belt high. If I didn't get it, I might walk, or I'd go with plan B after two strikes and just make good contact. I did get it. There are no curves or forkballs or sliders in slow-pitch softball. You know where a pitch is going the instant it leaves the pitcher's hand, and if it is heading where you want it to, you grip the bat more firmly and wait patiently for the ball to arrive. This waiting is precisely what causes pop flies—that softball looks like a watermelon coming at you in slow motion, and you make the decision to swing long before the muscles need to start coaxing the bat around. It is these perfect pitches, the ones you wait for, into which you channel all your energy, and often just a split second too soon because it's so hard to wait for the glory and limousines and super-models that you can so plainly visualize. I got my pitch, and I waited, and I swung. And whether it was the extra weight of our mascot stitched on my leading arm or something else, the bat did not arrive early. I made solid contact, and sent a hard ground ball right up the middle. I rounded first base as the center fielder scooped up the ball, and turned back toward the bag with a very satisfied feeling.

The next batter was my administrative partner and cofounder of the tortoise club; we were among the slowest members of the team. Our foot speed can best be clocked with sundials. He and I always joked that we would have a footrace someday, but someday didn't really give us enough time. If he got on base, the team would be relying on two of its slowest runners to cross the plate with insurance runs. He was a clutch hitter, though. All he had to do was get it out of the infield and we could probably both advance a base—anything stopped short of the outfield grass was almost certainly a double play. He knew this too, and with the authority of an angry gay robot crashing through buildings and stomping on cars, he laced a line drive down the third base line into left field. Had he hit it a little softer, it would have been a double, but it got to the left fielder so fast that he still had a chance to make a double play against us. Fortunately, we galumphed safely into first and second base, and there we stood as we heard the excited cheers from our dugout and watched the next batter stroll to the plate. He was one of the guys we had agreed to recruit as we sat around the bar table the previous winter, one of the *fleet*. He was a good hitter, too.

This kind of moment does not present itself very often in life, and it was very difficult not to get swept away in the emotion and start doing the robot dance on second base. I kept my wits and thought about what I would do when he made contact with the ball. I had to be deliberate but quick because this game could very likely be determined at this at bat. Anything on the ground, of course, and I would take off . . . using the term very liberally. Anything in the air to straight right field and I would take a big lead because the more visible play for the right fielder would be back to first base once a catch was made. Anything in the air to left or center and I would cautiously move off the bag and let instinct take over. It was not the late summer heat that was making me sweat.

I believe that the batter fouled the first pitch down the third base line into a tree, but I don't think there were any other pitches before he got the pitch he had waited for. He hadn't just waited for this pitch since stepping to the plate; he had waited for it all season. He turned on it and drove it high in the air to left field. As the ball left the bat, I left the bag and watched as it arced over my head. I remember it in slow motion, almost straight above me against the twilight sky. It was going to go deep and so I kept trotting until I was halfway between second and third. At that point, I knew that I was going to score because nobody was going to catch it, but I did not know quite how far the ball would travel. So I kept watching it as it sailed first over the head of the left fielder, and then finally over the fence in left field. Our opponents had their last at-bats still ahead, but I knew the game was over even before I reached third base, and I think everyone else did, too. I slapped hands with the third base coach, crossed the plate, and turned to congratulate the two runners behind me.

Throughout the buzz as this unfolded, I think that many of us could hear Kurt Gowdy or Vin Scully calling the whole at bat over an old transistor radio in dad's garage:

Runners on at first and second, one out here in the top half of the final inning. They are clinging to a one-run lead—not the speed you want on the bases in a situation like this, but they'll take the insurance any way they can get it. It's been a long road to this moment, let's see if they've got anything left in the tank.

(Any one of a host of color commentators butts in . . .): You know, they told me in the hotel elevator this morning that the guy stepping to the plate played Division-I ball in college and actually considered a professional career at one point, so they may not have the speed on the bases, but they have the right guy coming to the plate.

They acquired him during the offseason for just such a moment. The outfield knows it, and they are playing him straightaway and deep—anything gets by and runs start ticking on the scoreboard. Here's the pitch . . . swing! and a foul ball lobbed softly into the left field grandstand, out of play.

Color Commentator: That looked a lot like a slow, arcing pitch—they haven't really been mixing it up a whole lot tonight. I don't think it fooled him, but I think he was just a little hungry. Either way, he tipped his cards and they're going to play him to pull the ball now. You can see the outfielders shading toward left.

Batter steps out of the box to collect himself, now digs in again and is ready. Here's the 0–1 delivery. . . . Swing. . . . AND A DEEP DRIVE TO LEFT FIELD! WAY BACK! They're gonna give chase but that . . . ball . . . is . . . GONE!! A monster three-run blast in the top of the seventh! And that one cleared everything!

Color Commentator: Yeah, including the bases. Heh heh. . . .

Shut up. That should just about sew this one up. That was far and away the biggest hit of the season for this team . . . actually the biggest hit in quite a few years. It wasn't a walk-off, but it may as well have been. Look at the celebration at home plate and in the dugout, and then at the long faces in the field, and you can toss out your score sheets. Three runs across on a mammoth home run here in the seventh, and that is a dagger in the heart of the odds-on favorite all season long. My, oh my!

In a breach of journalistic etiquette, this transcript has been reproduced *without* the express written consent of Cambridge League Baseball.

As if that wasn't enough, the very next batter stepped up to the plate and drove a ball over the center fielder's head. There was no fence in center field, so the ball kept rolling, and our guy kept running. He rounded third base and was waved home, but the ball was on its way. Sensing a play at the plate, which didn't quite materialize, he dove head first with arms outstretched and landed. Is say "landed" because he didn't really slide across the plate; he just landed, a belly flop, and stopped. His path had taken him 99 percent of the way around the base path, but he was stopped cold, about three feet from the plate. The ball was still on its way, so he did what came naturally. He made my crippled flounder routine in right field earlier in the season look like the Boston Ballet. The best way to put it is that he flopped the remaining three feet to home plate . . . to say that he crawled would be too generous. But he beat the throw. Even better than gravy, it was a thick, thick layer of icing on a lavish and decadent cake. And with that, we took a five-run lead into the bottom of the seventh.

It turned out to be a good thing that we had padded our lead. Our opponents scored a couple of runs and had runners on first and second with two outs. Another ball over the fence would tie the game. Here was the call:

Two on, two out, and two already across here in the bottom of the seventh. Down to the final out of their season, but they are not going down easy. One swing could keep this one going. The outfield is playing in the next county—they'll give up a base hit, but nothing more than that. Whatever happens, this has been one for the ages. Hold your breath, here comes the pitch. . . .

Color Commentator: It looks like another slow, arcing pitch, a lot like all the—(PUNCH!) Hey! Why did you do th—(PUNCH!)

Swing, and a line shot down the third base line!—this is troub—Oh! She spears it off the second hop! She got it! Now it's a footrace to the bag . . . and she's there! Ballgame! They did it! Can you believe what you just saw!? Look at the jubilation and disbelief down on the field. . . . Here's a team that came from worst to beat the first and just completed the most stunning upset we've seen in a long time. And for that, they will have a chance to play their long-time nemesis for the crown tomorrow night!

We'll be here, and I'm sure you will to. The pregame show will start at noon with season highlights, player interviews, and an in-depth look at some of the off-field scandals that dotted the season. Game time is at seven o'clock Eastern, four Pacific, right here on. . . .

Color Commentator: Hey, what'd I miss?

Coach Krzyzewski also wrote in his book *Leading with the Heart*, "When you cleanse yourself of a big victory, you may open yourself up to the opportunity for an even bigger victory." We cleansed ourselves with more than a few buckets of Pabst that night and went home to wait for our next opportunity.

A mediocre amateur sociologist once quipped, "(Nemeses) are to be kept mysteriously distant and are to reappear sporadically throughout life to offer fleeting opportunities for the oppressed to stand and deliver. Those who are not primed and ready for these chances will be blindsided every time." It was frustrating, and yet it was also the only way it really could have been. After all we had accomplished to make it to the championship game, the team that now stood ready to squash us was the team that we simply could not defeat, our nemesis. I cannot recall a game in which we scored even half of the runs they scored, and they had trounced us so soundly each of the last five times we had met that the trophy had probably already been engraved. The only difference this time was that we had done the impossible just twenty-four hours ago, and the seventh-inning home run was replaying itself over and over in our minds. We knew that these final two games were a lot more than just gravy: they were the whole succulent turkey, stuffed to the bursting point and surrounded by mounds of sweet, sweet cranberry sauce and creamy mashed potatoes . . . with the gravy. Whatever the outcome of the game, we would not be blindsided this time.

Both teams started arriving at the field about an hour before game time. We assembled in the third-base dugout, they in the first-base dugout. We wore the same shirts from the night before, still smeared with dirt and sweat, but adorned with our proud hero. We stole glances at our foe across the infield and didn't so much see a softball team as we saw the Soviet hockey team, the New York Yankees, Phi Slamma Jamma, the East German women's swim team.

Although nobody said the words, many of us realized what a singular memory this game would be in our lives. Many players on the team had never won a championship in any sport at any level, including myself. In fact, I had only ever played in one champion-ship game in my life, in an intramural floor hockey league in college. We lost by one goal, and all the gravy in the world couldn't drown the angst that had followed me onto every court and field and diamond ever since. This softball game was bigger than it was.

Before the game, the umpire inspected the bats in both dugouts to ensure that they complied with league regulations. Our rules permitted aluminum bats and aluminum wrapped with graphite for extra stiffness, but not "double wall" bats. Double wall bats are aluminum with a concentric outer composite shell, with a very small air gap between the two materials. The air gap allows the composite to flex and spring back when the bat contacts the ball, and this can easily add fifty feet to a deep fly ball. Our bats were inspected first, and the umpire found no evidence of air gaps or pine tar or doping or coveting a maidservant or anything else unsavory. He then crossed the diamond to out opponent's dugout where he was presented with four bats for inspection. They, too, were deemed compliant. The lights came on around the field and it was time to play ball.

There are thousands of recreational softball leagues in this country. None of the games or highlights are recorded anywhere. The thrills and the close plays and the comebacks fade with the twilight; the games exist while they are being played. There are no reporters, no cameras, no beer vendors. Fans are generally limited to blood relatives who attend the game out of a sense of duty, spite (depending on the caliber of the combatant to whom they are related), or fear of recrimination. There are simply two teams, a ball, some gravel, some bats . . . and a passion for a game whose metaphors weave through almost every aspect of American life and language. "He struck out." "He scored." "He hit one out of the park." "The preacher balked during the blessing." "It's the bottom of the ninth." "He's in a slump." "He went in standing up." Well, ok, most of the metaphors relate to sex or pressure, synonyms in my experience, but perhaps this discovery goes a long way toward explaining the passion and verve that people bring to the ball field on hot summer nights. On this night and on this field, a lot of people were trying to do something they had never accomplished and may never have a chance to do again. It was not very different than any other recreational league championship game—a magnified experience and, for an hour, the only game anywhere that mattered. I suppose that the differentiator was the fact that we had played this team so many times, and had never even come close to beating them.

Being the underdog by virtue of our regular season records and by our lamentable history with our opponent, we were up to bat first. Our leadoff man was the guy who had sealed the game the previous night with the towering home run over the left field fence. With slightly less flair for the dramatic after all the press conferences and Pabst, he watched four balls land well away from the plate and took a base on balls. Apparently the "scout," a diminutive replica of Tony Soprano, had called his pitcher into his office for a little chat—anything over the plate to this guy and he could expect a horse's head under the blankets in the morning.

Now, a base on balls is a fairly innocuous thing, but *Tiny* Soprano didn't do his homework this time. To combat the rampant problem in co-ed leagues of walking the men to get to the women, the league adopted a somewhat controversial rule aimed at stifling gender-based defense. In what some see as affirmative action gone awry and others see as a direct insult to female talent, our league gives special dispensation to women who step to the plate immediately after a man has walked. The rulebook is very clear on the subject:

If thou walkest a man with four balls,[2] that man may hence
proceedeth to first base, as it shall be endowed and bequeathed
unto him, and to his sons and grandsons after him. If, in turn,
this man is followed immediately by a maiden fair,[3] such maid-
en may either elect to striketh at the ball with the bat or may
proceedeth directly to first base with flowing hair gleaming as
the sun setteth, in which case, the man may proceedeth directly
to second base. Alternatively, the maiden may demandeth remu-
neration in the form of four young calves, three sheaves of bar-
ley, two prized oxen, and one manservant, to be selected from
the bullpen stock.

Our leadoff man, who had walked and now stood proudly on first
base, was followed in the lineup by a maiden fair. As she strolled
out of the dugout, her hair gleaming in the setting sun, we all
expected her to trot down the first base line and claim her prize (not
the livestock, the base). As she grabbed a bat on her way, we
tripped over each other trying to race to the fence and remind her
that she had a free pass to first base. We would have had runners on
first and second, with no outs, against our nemesis in the championship game. But she turned toward us, a little tentatively, and said, "I
want to hit."

As I've noted, any good nemesis will tell you that their primary
tactic is simply to wait for their opponents to defeat themselves in
their moment of opportunity. We hadn't expected our opportunity
to come so early in the game, but here was a statistically guaranteed
chance to have two runners on with nobody out, and our maiden
was going to play lower odds that she could achieve the same thing,
but with more dignity. It was her prerogative. The rules are very
clear, but our stomachs and hearts switched places as she stepped

---

2. Not "a man with four balls," but rather, four pitches that are balls.
3. The maiden need not be a virgin, but it is ok if she is.

into the batter's box and cocked the bat back against her shoulder. Even the calves and the oxen paced nervously in their holding pen.

> When what to our wondering eyes then appeared,
> But the counter-conclusion to what we had feared,
> A slow, arcing pitch sailed over the plate,
> She swung straight and true, not too soon, not too late,
>
> Her bat didn't waver, the ball didn't yield,
> It seared through the infield and into left field,
> And what happened next? Well, in Who-ville they've heard,
> That the runner on first ran past second to third.
>
> So to spite the affirmative rule that upset her,
> She'd played how she wanted, and done even better!
> The smile she brandished was one for the ages,
> A prelude, of sorts, to the rest of these pages. . . .

And with that, the tenor of the game was firmly established. We were going to take it to 'em that night the way Valvano's Wolfpack took it to top-ranked Houston in 1983, or the way Rollie Massimino's eighth-seeded Villanova Wildcats took it to mighty Georgetown in 1985, or the way the Boston Red Sox took it to the New York Yankees in 2004. Both runners scored, and after the first few innings, we had a 4–0 lead. Our nemesis wandered into their dugout, dazed and confused—they didn't know what had hit them.

But the game was only a few innings old. Global warming takes a long time. Winning a World Series in Boston or Chicago takes even longer. Getting to first base with a pretty girl can take forever. Lead changes in a softball game, however, happen quickly. No sooner had we built a comfortable early lead, than it was gone. Halfway through the game, we trailed 5–4.

It was about this time that one of our players happened to glance over at our opponent's dugout. Where there had previously been four bats leaning up against the fence for the pregame inspection, there were now at least eight. Knowing that this team had a reputation for using illegal bats, we duly notified the umpire, who all but shrugged it off. As it happened, he had forgotten to bring the list of approved and illegal bats with him, so in his mind, if it was long and straight and partially metallic, it was certified. George Brett would have loved this guy. We didn't have quite the pine tar meltdown that he did, but we voiced our displeasure, had insults hurled at us by our opponents, and walked back to our positions. They were cheating, and everybody on the field that night knew it . . . except the umpire, and possibly the color commentator. The swagger had shifted, and if we were going to win the game, we needed it back. It did not take long for an opportunity to materialize.

With a runner in scoring position, one of their batters . . . that is, one of their bats . . . hit a deep fly ball that split a gap in the outfield. Once again, the imagined iconic voices of baseball:

> Up next, two sisters who were in love with the same man, and each other, and found out about it in a very uncomfortable way. We'll have all three in the studio to slug it out and—

Oops, wrong channel. . . .

> Now there's a deep drive into left-center field! This will probably score a run. They're waving him in, and here comes the throw—cutoff by the shortstop and he fires it home—we're gonna have a play at the plate!—throw is a little offline—the pitcher stabs it backhand, whirls to his right and throws himself back toward the plate . . . and. . . . He got 'im! He's out! What a play! There's no objection from the runner—let's see how close that was in the replay . . . oh, no question, he was out by about a foot. And here comes the swagger right back through the door.

The play-by-play guy was right, although I do not recall giving my express written consent to use the swagger theme in their broadcast. Regardless, those mysterious bats might just as well have been kindling in the fire that started with "I want to hit," and this play at the plate was the spark that relit it.

I do not remember how we got the lead back. I doubt I had anything to do with it because my hits in this game included a swinging bunt to the pitcher and a menacing bouncer that rolled to a stop just shy of the shortstop. But we did retake the lead in the very next inning. We could tell by glancing in our opponents' dugout that they were in disbelief, and that they were angry. They were arguing with each other. They were calling us names. They couldn't figure out why this was happening. More than anything else, it was our renewed bravado and their inability to get past their disbelief that carried us into the bottom of the seventh inning with a three run lead, 9–6.

The first batter grounded out. We were two outs away from a championship. The second batter hit a high pop fly that stayed in the infield. I watched from right field as our shortstop, the same guy who had hit the home run the night before, cleared everyone within a three-mile radius away with "I got it! I got it! I got it! I got it!" He got it. One out away.

I was not supposed to be in right field, or any other field, during this last inning. It had been my turn to sit on the bench as we rotated our five outfielders four at a time into the field. But the guy whose turn it was to play right field had the innings confused and assured me it was my turn, and I couldn't talk him out of it. So I put on my glove and trotted out to right field to count the clovers, since nothing much usually happens there.

One out away. The batter stepping to the plate was the guy who had watched us from the stands the previous night, scouting our hitters and fielders and cheering for us with an unbridled flamboyance. We were the team that would roll over and play dead, and he had announced to the world that he couldn't wait.

Some of the members of our team have since expressed regret that we did not videotape the final game. It certainly would be great fun to watch it again, to recall all of the plays and little things that occurred along the way that got lost in the magnitude of the event and the excitement of the final inning. But some memories are better left alone, to ferment over time like good wine, or in our case, cheap beer. Seeing the game on video might remind us that it was just a group of friends playing softball on a neighborhood field on a nice evening in the late summer. That's not so bad, I suppose, but it's all right if our memories recall the event the same way we imagined it as ten- and twelve-year-olds, with fifty-thousand fans pumping their fists in the air at the same moment, with announcers calling the final few outs with brewing intensity and emotion, with camera shots of all the players grinning at each other in the field as we sensed what was happening, and perhaps even a blimp in the sky to send the overhead shots around the country. It's a long way from a sand lot to a major league park, but only in reality.

All of this brings us back to that ball drifting down through the September sky, passing through the lights that ringed the field. After fouling off the first two pitches, and bringing his team to within one strike of defeat, the batter got under a pitch and lifted a fly ball into right field. It is one of those moments you act out in the backyard over and over as a child—the chance to make the last play of a championship game. A friend once told me that his son hit a winning single in a Little League championship game but forgot to run to first base amidst the joyous celebration with his teammates. The outfielder threw the ball to first, the runner was out, and the winning base hit morphed painfully into the final out. It was little league, but this guy will carry that around with him for the rest of his life. I, too, would remember this moment vividly for the rest of my life, for better or worse, but I suppose that this is exactly what I had wanted earlier in the season—a chance to make a slightly more graceful and memorable play in right field, since nothing much usually happens out there.

I drifted to my right. The center fielder was converging on the ball, too, but it was hit mostly in my direction and I got under it first. I distinctly remember the lights in the background as it drifted down toward me. I opened my glove high above my head. . . .

"Do you believe in miracles?"

4

MAGIC BALL

Many people I know claim that baseball is a game of failure. A batter who hits successfully three times out of ten is considered to be at the top of the game. Striking out is common. Fielding errors are recorded and accumulated as team and individual statistics to the point at which professional games are witnessed by an adjudicator who determines if a misplayed ball is the fault of the fielder or not. I tend to look at the game differently and always have. Baseball is a game of belief, of second chances, and respect. And trust me, coaches—if you happen upon a sudden windfall of $3.99, do I have a deal for you.

When my daughter turned five years old and discovered that she could swing a baseball bat with speed and accuracy, she wanted to play. The kids all start with tee-ball, a study in inertia; stationary objects remaining so, and moving objects and children never stopping. Then most girls migrate to softball while the boys play baseball. Not Ellie. She knew from the time she was three years old and smacking beach balls clear across the living room and over the sofa (a home run) that she'd be playing with the boys, just like her brother. And so I agreed—wanted—to coach her first team, a tee-ball team of kindergartners, all full of energy and the whimsical notion that they were already in the majors.

This was not my debut as a youth baseball coach. I had helped coach my son's teams for the past two years, first as an assistant coach for his tee-ball team. The job of an assistant coach on a tee-ball team can be summarized in just a few requirements; point at the ball when it moves, remind the players to chase it, and try to make sure nobody gets hurt. I was a miserable failure at all three. I hopped up and down when the ball was in play, called out double play combinations whenever the ball was hit on the ground, and watched an inattentive player take a ball to the stomach. Still, to them I was coach, or sort of coach. Sometimes I was "mister" and sometimes I was "dad" and sometimes I was "the tall one over there," but every once in a while I was "coach." I liked those once in a whiles.

And so the following year, when my son advanced through the primordial baseball ranks and the graciously static yet perpetually poorly adjusted tee was replaced by a squatting parent lobbing rubber balls at the miniature batters, I wanted the frontman position. I wanted to be the head coach. I had an impressive résumé. I played Cub Scout softball when I was seven years old. I played recreational softball as an adult. I have watched a lot of baseball on TV. And I had coached tee-ball. Well, sort of coached. The job was mine.

I quickly learned that I had an innate ability to teach kids how to make contact with a moving ball while swinging a bat, sometimes in the right direction. Beyond that, though, I knew very little about teaching fundamentals about baseball. Half of the team was terrified to catch the ball and would dive for cover with their glove trailing in an affectation of a reach. The only way to overcome this was to persuade them that a rubber baseball doesn't hurt. Sadly, this was a lie. It does hurt. Noses were bloodied, and tears were shed whenever two combatants (teammates) would warm up at practice by playing catch. But at least the kids who got hit weren't diving for cover all the time. Maybe this was progress, and maybe if I softened the balls. . . .

I drove one day to the sporting goods store and purchased a bucket of tennis balls. These, I thought, would hurt less. I tossed them to the kids and had them play catch with these new marvels. They stopped diving away. Then they stopped stepping away. They would sometimes catch the ball, or hit it. This was indeed progress, and I felt that progress should be rewarded. So I made another trip to the sporting goods store to purchase one more ball. This one was shiny, and red. It cost $3.99.

All that any coach or I can hope to offer any child is perhaps one skill, one bit of physical or emotional elegance that he or she can add to life's repertoire. Sometimes, perhaps, it is just one moment. I believe that each player shows up on the first day with one small miracle inside—a catch that they never thought possible, a hit into the outfield, a hand of friendship offered to another player on either team—something that they will remember when they return to school in the fall, and maybe longer. Just one thing. It is an esoteric coaching philosophy, one that would get me fired within a week from any paid position, but it has never once failed me through six seasons of coaching youth baseball.

There was the boy who started playing baseball in third grade, having never held a bat. In his first game he took thirty-seven strikes before making contact, and so we taught him how to swing during our next practice by having him hit a hundred balls directly into a fence three feet away. We collapsed the game into a palpable space, and the batter's box became familiar. He hit the ball into the outfield four times in the next game, on just about four swings. That was his season, in an evening. Then there was the boy who was terrified to run to the next base, even first base, and so we ran with him base by base until one day he said, "You can stay back, coach," and he did it on his own. And there was Ellie, my daughter, who, after she had decided to play baseball with the boys instead of softball with the girls, would become anxious at times because of this decision. She was a good hitter, but hadn't yet learned to catch well, and so we worked on this for a season during practice and at home in the driveway and in the living room after dark until the day she caught an infield popup and doubled off the runner at second base. Sometimes the tiny miracle is an athletic achievement, but sometimes it is something else.

At the end of each game I would assemble the dusty players by the dugout and talk to them about the game, highlighting the things we did well and what we would work on at the next practice. And then I would toss the reward for progress, the shiny red baseball, to the player who had exemplified the most progress since the last game. It began as something of a lark, a simple idea to get the kids to settle down after a game and listen to a few rambling remarks that I might have. But the ball is red, it is round, and it is shiny, and I had not had these virtues fully appraised before bestowing this honor on the town's youth. It was this whimsical notion that a small gleaming reward might compel a group of first graders to work toward an achievement that converted the red baseball into the Red Ball. The transformation bordered on transubstantiation, and the ball became more spirit than object. The sacredness and ceremony of handing the Red Ball to each week's recipient morphed into something quite liturgical, as they cupped it in their hands and promised solemnly to return it at the beginning of the next game. I was mystified, but still a bit dissatisfied with the symbolism, mystical or literal as it was. Most of the time I was awarding athletic achievement, even if it was masked beneath the guise of progress. Neither of these are original sin, of course, but there was more than a little red luster missing from the sheen. The Red Ball was not yet associated with the best miracles.

And so I thought about what this sacred relic could come to symbolize, if its true value in a young life was equal to its perception of value. Most of the kids will not play baseball for more than a few more years, but they will always, always be interacting with people, both friend and foe. These simplifications never really dissolve, do they? Maybe the Red Ball could be reconsecrated as a symbol that these kids could remember for a few more of life's innings. Perhaps it could stand for sportsmanship—civility. Perhaps it could stand for grace—quiet perseverance. Perhaps it could stand for teamwork—trust and respect.

Whenever I consider these traits, I tip my hat to a pitcher named Armando Galarraga, and I use his character and his story to explain them to the kids. I saw him pitch in a minor league game in Oklahoma City one hot summer night, five innings of shutout baseball and nearly a no-hitter before yielding a half dozen runs in the sixth and strolling dolefully into the showers. But a few years prior to this, he had pitched for the Detroit Tigers, at a home game. He carried a perfect game into the ninth inning, with two outs. At the time, the number of perfect games in the entire recorded history of Major League baseball registered in the low twenties. The home crowd and even the visiting fans were on their feet, as was much of

our culture. Each player has within them a miracle. He reared back
and delivered the final pitch, which was bounced sharply to the first
baseman. Galarraga darted over to cover first base, the first baseman tossed him the ball, and he tagged the bag a full step ahead of
the runner. A perfect game.

. . . Except that the runner was called safe. The earth stopped
spinning for a moment in disbelief and denial. The crowd was
apoplectic. Watching the game on television, so was I. I think I
remember jumping up and down and pointing to the screen so that I
could explain to the umpire the error of his ways. Everybody expected Galarraga to assault the man in some fashion.

Instead, he looked stunned for just a second. Then, his body
slackened and he smiled, not at anybody in particular, but to himself, and to the miracle he knew had just happened. He gathered his
strength and strode calmly back to the mound, reared back and got
the next batter out, and in doing so he accomplished something that
had never before been done, and will never be repeated. He pitched
a perfect game plus one; twenty-eight outs in a row instead of
twenty-seven. The City of Detroit showered him with accolades.
The umpire made a tearful televised apology. The miracle was
memorialized in the consciousness of baseball, if not its record
books. But what I remember was his grace, his civility. There were
only two or three hundred people in attendance in Oklahoma City
the night of his minor league performance, and I entertained no-
tions of drifting by the dugout in between innings so that I might
look him in the eye and thank him for one of baseball's most
profound moments. But it wasn't his night, and he hit the showers
before I got up the nerve to shuffle my way over.

The year of Galarraga's miracle was the second year of coaching
my son's team, and I began using it as an example. And it was this

iconic moment that led me, between seasons, toward a clearer resolution to reshape the Red Ball spirit the following year, when my daughter would take the field for the first time. I first confirmed that such a broad and liberal reinterpretation of a small red institution would not require a revisionist doctrine or the deconstruction of any creeds, and was pleased that as yet, no elders nor deacons nor bishops of the game had the faintest idea what I was doing.

And so it was that I found myself coaching in my third year, fronting a team of five-year-olds, including my daughter, playing tee-ball. Having seen many such youth show up to practice ready to bat in front of forty thousand people only to fight off tears when they first step to the plate in front of two dozen strangers, I was eager to see how Ellie would shoulder the spotlight. Perhaps with an equal amount of fatherly vigor, I was eager to test my new, kinder, gentler coaching philosophy, or theology, or whatever it was. On the Saturday morning of our first game in early May, I arrived in the parking lot with her, wondering how gracefully her shy, tiny (but sensationally speedy) being would absorb the monumental aspect of the impossibly flat green expanse of field bespeckled with an opposing team dehumanized by the color of their shirts. It's the blue team today.

This was the first organized baseball game of Ellie's life. I think she had worn her bright orange uniform to bed the night before. Today was her day, her day to become a player, just like her older brother, just like her dad used to be, just like the Red Sox she liked to watch (though she would quickly forsake this allegiance in favor of the Orioles, what with their name on her jersey and the insinuated franchise connection). We were the first to arrive, and curiously, we remained the only ones to arrive for quite some time. I looked hopefully around. It was hard to see very far because of the nickel-sized hailstones pelting the earth and the black cloud that had descended from on high to blot out all vestiges of morning sunlight.

"Where is everyone?" I muttered.

"Uh, Dad, there's lightning. And hail."

"Well yeah, but. . . ."

Eventually, another car pulled up alongside ours and a man opened his window. It was the other coach, with a blue player strapped carefully into the back seat. We shared the despondent look of young boys who had just lost their puppy or their iPod, and our misplaced hope asked, "Do you think we can maybe get this one in?" Eventually, we acquiesced to powers greater than baseball, exchanged condolences, and drove away as the hail beat resolutely against our tin-can cars. Ellie and I continued driving all the way to Fenway Park that day, determined to find a game. It was the last day that these local roustabouts would be her favorite team. Her heart turned southward toward Baltimore, and there it has remained. She was an Oriole. That never bothered me. Kids should find and keep their own allegiances.

Days later, we eventually got to play, and at the end of the game I solemnly awarded the Red Ball to the player who best exemplified the concepts of teamwork or sportsmanship, my new theology. It took about three games for the kids to learn that this prized accolade was not awarded for the best play or the longest hit, but for helping someone out of the dirt, congratulating another player, working hard without frustration, or simply trusting a teammate. Again, each ceremony was attended by the reverence in the eyes and hands of the recipient, who would take it for the everlasting interstitial time between games, affix his or her signature, and dutifully return it to me immediately upon arrival at the field for the next game so that the next deserving player could grasp it. (As it is, shiny red baseballs are extremely rare this far north, and so a single ball must last a season. It travels from player to player like Lord Stanley's Cup, but costs less and may be handled safely without white cotton gloves). It became the greatest highlight of any game.

What I enjoyed most, so much that it even choked me up once or twice, was bringing the kids in after the game to take a knee and explaining why I was awarding the Red Ball that night. I would mix in a few clues: "This player still cheered even when we were down by eleven runs," or "This player made some great catches and some not so great almost-catches, but each time got right back into the ready position and prepared for the next play," or "This player walked over to help an injured opponent." Slowly, each player would begin to recognize who it was that I was talking about, and look over at the person with genuine pride in their eyes. There was never, not once, an "Aw, man!" or "What about me, coach?" Not once. When they figured out who I was talking about, they would start cheering for that player, and that was my cue to place the ball in a hand outstretched from a disbelieving smile, speak the player's name, and say simply, "Well done."

One morning, the team took its customary knee on the grass in front of me. There had been a hit with bases loaded to take the lead. That same player had come in to pitch the final out and preserve that one-run lead. There had been a successful pitching debut, and some grand glove work in the field. But when I asked rhetorically who would get today's Red Ball, the question was answered before I could even finish the question. One of the boys piped up with the name of another boy, and I paused and asked him to repeat it. He did, and he was joined by a chorus of young voices all chanting the name. He hadn't been the pitcher that day, nor had he laced the line drive that scored the go-ahead run. But he had been the first to congratulate the pitcher who made a successful debut, and the first to begin the cheer for that batter. The others had taken notice, and today's Red Ball was awarded by the whole team, not just me. "They get it," I keep reminding myself.

Each player on the team gets the ball at least once. Sure, I keep an eye out toward the end of the season for deserving gestures from the kids who haven't had it yet, but each player does something to deserve it. By the end of the year, every player on the team has signed the ball. As much as I would love to keep a lineup of auto-graphed Red Balls on my mantle, I decided that each one really belongs in the hands or on the mantle of a player most deserving throughout the season. The first Season Red Ball went to the first kid who reached it after I heaved it into center field after our last game. This was a mistake, and it was precisely at this moment that the idea of the most deserving player first crystalized as an alterna-tive to the assault and battery that nearly ensued. More than one parent cast a disapproving look at me, formulating the language for the lawsuit over the concussions and broken arms that were now so imminent. Fortunately, a child emerged unscathed from the rubble and held the Red Ball aloft to the heavens. It was his. But I knew I should rethink my end of season policies, partly for consistency with the endowed symbology of the ball, and partly to stay out of prison.

And so the next year, I awarded the Season Red Ball to a young boy who had run for the very first time in his life after hitting a single during one of our games late in the season. He had sustained a paralyzing injury as an infant, but had spent his entire life regath-ering his strength and smiling. Actually, I didn't award the ball.

The team did. On the day of the final game, I received word that this boy would be away with his family that night and would not be able to join the team. I was disappointed, but tee-ball contracts typically include no clauses of exclusivity over other social obligations or entanglements. And so we played with seven that night instead of eight, but seven with a unified voice. At the end of the game, when I asked the team to huddle around on the infield grass and take a knee, I told them how proud I was of each of them for standing in front of a lot of people and being brave enough to swing their bats, for swinging the bats only at the ball and not at each other, for learning how to trust and respect themselves and their friends, and for learning that in baseball, you always get a second chance if you believe you will. It is hard to know how much of the world is absorbed with clarity in the minds of five- and six-year-olds—probably more than we think. On this night they reminded me that they are deserving of our faith. When I asked them who they felt was most deserving of the Season Red Ball, to a player they spoke the name of the boy who had worked the hardest to overcome the most and achieve his miracle, smiling the whole time.

Then a few years later, I awarded the Season Red Ball to a boy who had worked so hard to be able to pitch but couldn't quite reach the plate. He kept the Red Ball where he could see it through the winter, practiced as much as he could, and came back the next season for his pitching debut; a perfect first inning (one-ninth, almost, of Galarraga's opus, but equally rare at this level), and a shutout second inning.

Youth baseball seasons come and go quickly. The one in which the Red Ball became a living thing had begun with the grand disappointment of the hail storm that we could have *almost* played through. A great deal happened in the span of six weeks in the spring of that year. My daughter played her first baseball game and cast aside many layers of self-doubt. I pulled a muscle playing catch with a five-year-old. Each of the kids on the team earned the Red Ball and got to take it home. Some slept with it on their pillows, others took it to school in their backpacks or on weekend family excursions. Coaches, trust me. If you happen upon a sudden windfall of $3.99, there is not better way on earth to spend it.

5

THE TIMING PATTERN

Break *hard off the line of scrimmage.* It was a new play that we had started practicing in the street as we walked to the game. *Shoot straight downfield, eyes forward. After you cross the line, curl inward just enough to look back over your right shoulder. The ball will be right there.*

Until Tom Brady and Adam Vinatieri arrived in Massachusetts, the most famous play in the history of New England football had been Doug Flutie's last second Hail Mary touchdown pass for Boston College in 1984. It won a big game against the Miami Hurricanes, solidified the Heisman Trophy for Flutie, and inscribed the play into Jesuit doctrine as an alternate definition of its namesake, or so I've been led to believe. It was arguably one of the most exciting plays in college football history, or the history of sports, for that matter. It replays over and over anytime a television network counts down the top ten finishes of all time, usually right before or right after the Stanford trombone player flirts with the afterlife. The whole play has become one of the most exalted images of college football, the heave, the ball slicing through the mob of defenders, the receiver falling backward behind all of them with the ball in his grasp, and Flutie being lifted toward the heavens. Now . . . name the guy who made the catch.

I had to look it up. It was Gerard Phelan, a senior, who after the game claimed that he "held onto it like it was my first newborn." Phelan was caught in the undertow of maroon and gold jerseys in the end zone, and that was almost the last anybody ever heard of him. His name drifted into obscurity as a supporting actor among the annals of sporting's greatest moments. This moment was Flutie's. He was the kid from nearby Natick whose charisma overcame his height and whose talent legitimized Boston as a national college football venue. And while he had virtually assured himself of the Heisman Trophy before "the play," the name *Flutie* owes a great deal of its luster to Gerard Phelan.

The Flutie-to-Phelan Hail Mary was not, of course, the only biblical legacy in the game of football. Franco Harris of the Pittsburgh Steelers, normally a running back, rebounded a ricocheted pass and ran the ball into the endzone in what has become the hallowed *Immaculate Reception*. Notre Dame fielded an apocalyptic backfield in 1924 that became known as the *Four Horsemen*. Someday, a player will be nicknamed *Amazing Grace*. It should have been Lynn Swann, but the smooth resonance of his name as it was spoken and the obvious allusion to the most graceful of beings was enough.

Yet however divine or cataclysmic a team's twelfth player may be, finding and catching a football that is rock hard from its speed and rotating more often than not on more than one axis requires exceptionally strong and graceful hands. Doing it among the outstretched and flailing arms of defenders who can run ten yards in one second is left to the blessed few upon whom have been bestowed superhuman foot speed, reflexes that defy both Newtonian and relativistic physics, and an extrasensory connection with the superhuman at the other end of the pass. Imagine what the rest of us could do in our jobs if we possessed such extraordinary qualities!

Strong and graceful. I have always wanted to be a great wide receiver, and I actually possess better-than-average strength and grace in my hands, or at least I did twenty years ago. It is probably no slight subliminal coincidence, then, that I bestowed upon my children the wishes that they might inherit these two traits. The first words I ever spoke to my son when I held him in my hands were, "Live a strong life, Ben." The first words I spoke to my daughter when I held her were, "Live a graceful life, Ellie." I'll let the two of them translate these hopes however they wish, if they wish. Put the two of them together in a few years, though, and they could develop into a great wide receiver . . . if they inherit their mother's foot speed. A great receiver also needs speed, and my endowment here is *de minimus* in every sense and tense. I have always been slow when I run. I am still so slow that walking and trotting and running are not clearly distinguishable—I totter. I will be slow forever. A human being can improve speed, but not create it. A friend put it to me best. During a softball game, I hit a double, after which I waited patiently for the next batter to drive me in with a single. At my next plate appearance, I hit the ball through the left field gap, and circled the bases as the ball rolled deeper and deeper into the outfield (there was no fence). Upon returning to the dugout after the home run, I was greeted by my friend, our pitcher, who blithely observed, "You made it around the bases faster the first time."

My father was a star quarterback when he played high school football in Illinois in the 1950s. I was not. Not in Illinois or in any other state. I spent my after school hours singing in garage bands, which theoretically can yield comparable prestige and social opportunities, someday. I wanted to be a wide receiver.

My father's years as quarterback were legendary. In his first year, he led his team to its first undefeated season in the history of the school. He and his backfield replaced four graduating seniors, and by most standards, they were out of place. Dad anchored the crew at 175 pounds. His fullback weighed in at 165 pounds and actually wrestled in a weight class ten pounds lighter. One of the two halfbacks was a lineman by training (at least he was big), and the other was a speed skater who had never played football before and who weighed less than the fullback. This is to say that of the three running backs, two of them rivaled the body mass indices of the cheerleaders, one was a mule (no offense to other high school linemen), and one knew how to go around in counterclockwise circles for a long time. But notwithstanding their minimal mass and obvious inexperience, they became the Four Horsemen reincarnate on their very first play from scrimmage. They ran a straight T-formation, and Dad called the 22 Counter Trap in the huddle. The backfield started to the right, my father faked a handoff to the featherweight fullback, who continued to the right, then handed it to the lineman/halfback, who had cut back—the *counter*—to head straight through the line between the center and the right guard. The center and right guard kept the encroaching defensive linemen and linebacker from following the play to the right, but it was the key block—the *trap*—which prevented the left defensive guard from returning to his original position after being lured away by the en masse rightward shift. His starting point, opposite the center and right guard (the *2-hole*), was now a gaping hole. The halfback took the ball straight through and scuttled sixty yards straight downfield.

Had he been blessed with the speed of a halfback and not of a lineman, he would have made it to the endzone. As it was, he was tackled fifteen yards short of the goal line. It was the first time anyone had even touched him. The four friends never looked back and never lost a game that year. Twenty years later, my father and the halfback who ran that first play found themselves on the faculty of the same college in western Michigan. Legend has it that they memorialized their perfect season each fall by running the same play on the opening day of classes, throwing the key blocks against the first row of students and barreling down the classroom aisles to the back of the room before even handing out the syllabi.

To this day, fifty years later, their perfect season stands as the only undefeated season in their high school's history. They recently reunited at the school and donated their cleats to the display case.

I have no football memories as grand or as long-standing as this play, every detail of which was recounted to me with reminiscent zeal by my father fifty years after it was run. But at one point in my life, I did find myself on a team of apparent gridiron misfits. The difference was that during our memorable season (not our first season), we trailed by two touchdowns after the first two plays from scrimmage. But after that, my story begins to catch up and bear some slight resemblance to my father's. Let me back up a little.

On the days that my college buddies and I were not playing pickup basketball, we were tossing a football around on our school's state-of-the-art Astroturf football field. Playing on Astroturf requires heightened self-awareness of every joint from your hips to your ankles: where are they now and where would I like them to be in another step? Without training and discipline, Astroturf can dismantle the bodies of otherwise virulent young engineering students. This was not the Astroturf of today, which blends Easter grass with Kevlar. This was that thin scratchy carpet spread over concrete, with enough friction to easily snag hapless human limbs. It had a voracious appetite for our well-being. It caused concussions, whiplash, sprained ankles, damaged ligaments. But on the days that it caused no harm, it felt good. With less resistance than a grass field, and with a rut-free surface that sloped very gradually downward toward each sideline to promote drainage, we felt fast. An arthritic antelope could have outrun us, but we felt fast.

We resided eleven floors directly above the field in one of a cluster of high-rise dormitories that enclosed the south endzone in an arced array and created the illusion on the field of a huge enclosed stadium. Our school played 1–AA ball in the days when it was still called 1–AA. 1–AA schools don't play in enclosed stadiums, but between the Astroturf and the vertical façade around the south endzone, our imaginations never let us down.

On Saturday afternoons in the fall, we'd watch the games from high atop the field in our dorm rooms—our private luxury boxes. Our parents never caught on that the monstrous checks they wrote each fall for tuition, room, and board actually included season tickets and amenities usually not offered to those of college student affluence. On weeknights, when we should have been solving differential equations, we perched high above the same field and watched with great interest the intramural flag football games on the same field, where "tackles" were registered by removing flags tied to the ball carrier's waist. There were some good athletes in the intramural games, to be sure—guys who had played in high school, no doubt. But from eleven stories up, it looked easy. So, during our sophomore year, we registered a team from our dorm floor. Not a single one of us had played high school football, but we played against each other a lot whenever the mood hit us. The modest skills that we had were accentuated by the relative ineptitude of the group as a whole, so the guys who could throw generally threw pretty well, and the guys who could run or catch were highly touted within our circle of players. I had pretty good hands back then and usually managed to catch two or three touchdown passes during a pickup game. Playing on an intramural team was my chance to be a wide receiver in games that were actually recorded somewhere, kind of. We felt that we easily registered at the speed and talent level we had watched every night from our loft a hundred feet above the field.

We did not. One of my father's academic colleagues once described another colleague's mind as a "veritable cesspool" of trivial information. I doubt if any more apt commentary could be applied to our inaugural flag football season, though surely the phrase "transgression against the sport" should be given fair consideration. It was quite the opposite of my father's inaugural season, which was perfect. We were not undefeated. We were defeated and defeated and defeated . . . and defeated. I do not recall winning a single game or even coming close. I never caught a touchdown pass. We were so bad that bad things happened to us even between plays and after the games. I was ejected from a game on the grounds that I had used *sarcasm* when referring to an official who allowed a team of drunken fraternity brothers to use their own discretion when differentiating a snared flag from an assault. I actually had to schedule a meeting with some person of responsibility in the school's athletic department to explain myself and plead for reinstatement. It looked so easy from our luxury boxes, but on the turf the game moves much more quickly. Gaps open and close and patterns diverge and converge in split seconds. Like any sport, football has many levels. We learned that we were much better off watching even this very modest level from the secluded confines of our rooms.

My singular individual highlight of the season came on a drizzly night midway through a game that we lost thirty-five to nothing. We were playing a team called "the Doctors," a name that conferred upon them an affiliation with our medical school, we presumed. I have long contended that engineers (like us) ought to share the prestige and the salaries of medical doctors (like them)— think for a moment about wiping either profession from the face of the earth, throughout human history and forevermore. But alas, on this night the doctors were veritably the better breed. At some point in the game this realization rose quite plainly in my mind, and I got mad. One of my responsibilities on this team, in addition to my stoically hapless attempts at catching the ball that night, was to punt the ball whenever we needed to, which was often. I channeled all of my medical wrath and malevolence through my right leg (which, ironically, has since been examined, torqued, injected, and surgically repaired in many places by many doctors for many reasons) and sent the ball arcing and spiraling through the backlit drizzle. It landed more than fifty yards downfield after a beautiful flight. In the college or professional ranks, it would have been a thirty-five yard punt, measured from the line of scrimmage and subtracting the fifteen yards that the punter stands behind the line. An elite punter (pardon the oxymoron) who consistently kicks thirty-five yard punts is like an internist who routinely prescribes the wrong dosage of the right medicine; good honest try, but they will both be looking for work frequently. With some practice, conditioning, strength training, and coaching, though, I might have been able to kick that far with some consistency. And even a rational skeptic might agree that, benefiting from such training, I might have added five or six yards to my distance. Such credentials might have qualified me as a punter on a college team whose tradition and standards were rooted in the firmament of mediocrity. Yet regardless of standards, such a position on any team is fraught with more social and economic peril than almost any other profession in the Western world. Even when these guys go pro, they are paid less than most medical interns. They are called upon only when their team has failed, to try to minimize the damage. You will never see a punt on any countdown of the greatest or most memorable plays in sporting history. And punters must have aliases—they can never reveal their true identities to anyone for fear of the convulsive mirth that would certainly follow. Besides, I would have had to be angry with doctors all the time, and for athletes, such particular malice is generally unwise. I was very pleased with my thirty-five-yard malevolent punt, as it would have been measured officially, and have never again come close to matching that mark.

All things considered, it was not solely a lack of talent that thwarted our run. It was our lack of timing and toughness. Toughness? In flag football, where the prevailing risk is that your shorts might fall a few inches when the flag is ripped from its moorings? Suffice it to say that when a team of engineering students is running at full speed through a team of jocks, intellectual prowess earns very little respect. We were hit and hit hard. The rules prohibited tackling, blind blocks, or any contact other than face-to-face blocking at the line of scrimmage, but the officials (students themselves, mostly of the liberal arts, it seems) apparently suspended these rules for their own amusement whenever our team took the field. We became intimately acquainted with that Astroturf. There is probably a similar story, from another university, of slipshod athletes who banded together in their hallowed halls of kinetics and materials science, got their faces planted in the Astroturf, and rose from the dust and rug burns to design the new, more pampering and cushiony Astroturf used in today's modern stadiums. My hat is off to them, even if I only made them up. And what of us? Well, we chose the path less traveled. We came back for more.

Now we were trespassing. The first season's unfortunate efforts were spawned from ignorance. Now we knew we did not belong. But a curious, though stereotypical trait of engineers is that as a breed we usually do not accept failure without questioning its precursors and altering them. Clearly, there must be a way, a better way, to play the game competitively without the repetitious faceplants into the Astroturf. (Here is where a distraction into high-tech ways to make more comfortable Astroturf could have earned us millions of dollars and maybe even some girlfriends, but we chose to dwell on our own fallacies rather than the evolution of fake sod.) There had to be a better way to play. If we were to withstand those nosedives onto the carpet, we had to become tougher. If we wanted to avoid them, or at least reduce their frequency, we had to improve our timing and precision; we had to learn how to be where they weren't, when they weren't there. No more casual schoolboy play.

We found ourselves a practice field the next fall, or more precisely, it found us. My roommate and I moved into an apartment several blocks from the dormitories, in a quiet residential neighborhood. Across the street, next to a large shaded playground for children, was our field; lush grass lined by tall oak trees on one side and surrounded by a twelve-foot-high, well-maintained, black chain-link fence. This was not an empty lot; it was a scale model of a football field. It measured about fifty yards long and roughly half the width of a regulation field. The earth was soft, but the oak trees littered the far sideline with acorns that left imprints on your skin when you fell on them. The fence closed us in as if we were fighters in a ring or combatants on a hockey rink. The dimensions allowed deep patterns and a spread offense, but kept everybody close enough to ensure plenty of contact. There was never anybody else there on Sunday afternoons. It was perfect.

And so, every Sunday afternoon that fall, our team, along with some new recruits, would convene shortly after noon for however many hours it took to feel tougher. We played full contact tackle football without pads or helmets. We played purposefully until it hurt, and the pain usually lasted through Thursday. I was slammed down onto the acorns. We crashed into the fence, and each other. We sprained things. It was not a Bear Bryant making of men, but even he probably would have cracked half a smirk had he watched us from the shade of the oaks, even if half of that half smile was in muse. We got tough.

We also worked on advancing the ball. Toughness is good in a game of football, but it is just an ancillary benefit to any team that cannot move downfield. My roommate, Duke, was our quarterback. After classes most evenings, he and I would cross the street to our field and run pass patterns until either my legs or my lungs gave out. I was a literalist back then, though my worldview has relaxed somewhat now in middle age. But back then, we turned my literalism into an asset. "Take five steps downfield and cut across the middle" meant "take five steps downfield and cut across the middle." Some people use stones or bottlecaps to draw up the plays and patterns in the huddle. Duke always drew the plays with his finger on his shirt, directing three or four receivers to cross paths with each other. He let most of the guys get away with some broad interpretive latitude with his instructions, but not me. His obsessive-compulsive roommate would run his assigned pattern *exactly*. Five steps meant five steps, not four or six. Cutting across the middle meant straight across the middle, otherwise Duke would give me an angle. I was very obedient, and I became his preferred receiver because he always knew exactly where I would be. And like an obedient hound, I learned that if I was exactly where I was supposed to be and had gotten there exactly as I was supposed to, there would usually be a ball waiting for me. On those autumn evenings, I would run my patterns over and over, and Duke would loft, sling, and fire the ball downfield to me. We committed the plays to muscle memory and tried them out on Sundays.

Our favorite pattern was the out-and-up. I would line up just off the line of scrimmage and run ten yards straight downfield before cutting hard straight toward the sideline. That piece of the pattern itself is a well-known play that teams commonly use for short yardage. The defender usually plays off and hedges toward the center of the field, so cutting away from him immediately frees the receiver. If the ball is thrown to the outside, it is nearly impossible to defend, but there is no field left, and the receiver steps out of bounds or is tackled trying to cut upfield. What makes the out-and-up pattern so effective is that its first half, the *out*, is laced with one of the greatest temptations in all of sports. As the defender watches the play develop, he sees nothing but green earth (or Astroturf, whose aesthetic appeal is not at all diminished in this context) between himself and the goal line at the opposite end of the field. There is nobody except the receiver anywhere near him, and nobody would have an angle on him if he became the hunted instead of the hunter. An interception of an out pattern is a touchdown. When the ball is tossed, human instinct leads the defender to the path between thrower and catcher, which is exactly the wrong place to be if the ball is thrown well. It will already be in the receiver's hands when you get there, and now the receiver will have a free path upfield, leaving the stupefied defender roiling about what could have been. Disciplined defenders play the receiver, not the ball on an out pattern. But the defenders we played against, though substantially tougher and quicker than we were, were no more disciplined than schoolboys. The out-and-up play capitalizes on the most basic of human vices: greed. When the receiver is near the sideline, he turns back toward the quarterback, who fakes a pass. That is all it takes. The defender sees green fields and accolades ahead, and in the absence of any recent coaching, takes two steps into the envisioned pathway of the ball. When he realizes the pass was a fake, the receiver has already taken the same two steps in the opposite direction, away from the defender, and up the sideline— the *up*. In pickup football games, the play usually ends up as a touchdown, as long as it is not run too frequently. As a receiver, I always knew the play had worked long before I caught the pass. I knew it when the defender muttered "oh shit!" and scrambled to change directions while I made the deliberate turn upfield. As a defender, I knew the play had worked against me when I uttered the same thing. It is human instinct to go for the ball, every time, even when you know the play, and even before the ball is aloft. If a beautiful girl walks across your path, you look, every time. You follow with your eyes, sometimes much too long, until you either remember or realize that you cannot touch her, at which point you mutter something like, "Oh shit."

I broke rank only once while running a pass pattern, and was glad I did. But that is part of the story that emerged later, away from our small grassy enclave.

Our team strode onto the Astroturf on the first night of our second intramural season, stridently ready to meet it head on (the turf, that is, and the season too). We were also prepared to offer some resistance this time, having passed the early autumn drilling ourselves on precision and drilling each other with shoulders and forearms. I quietly told myself the same thing I always tell myself before any game in any sport against any team: "We can beat these guys. They don't know us." Speaking these words aloud can charge a team's spirit if voiced with discretion, though, of course, they may sometimes be frivolous or dishonest or even heretical. Forming the thought and letting it rise unspoken simply sets the jaw and is never improper. Quiet confidence is the purest bravado. It is believable, subliminally conspicuous, and relatively innocuous when it backfires. And it does backfire.

Our opponents were first to have the ball. On the very first play after the kickoff (which was nothing close to my fifty-yard miracle in the mist), they ran a simple pass play, which they completed. The receiver then blazed through and past our defense with speed hitherto unwitnessed by our eyes, which suddenly felt virginesque in perpetuity, as did the rest of our physiques. Ok, we thought, it was one bad play. Now it's our turn. We received the ensuing kickoff and returned the ball nearly to the thirty yard line; not bad—it was midfield on the diminished sixty-yard stretch of turf cordoned off for intramural league play. We huddled up under the lights and Duke called our first play, sketching its dynamics invisibly on his chest with his fingers. As we broke and stepped to the line of scrimmage, we faced the looming semicircular dormitories that arced around the south endzone, from where we had once dreamt of success and prestige on this very carpet. Time slowed down just a bit as the moment planted itself in my memory, but it sped up straightaway. I lined up wide to the left. The play was to me. Hike! I ran my route and turned to catch the ball, only to see a flash of a human being running in the other direction spear the ball with his hands, and tear down the field toward its lonely open end. He returned his interception for a touchdown, untouched.

Our masculinity lay shriveled on the carpet, trodden and trampled by the spiked feet of experience and prowess. Two plays into the game, we trailed by two touchdowns. Try to find a statistic like that, anywhere. We did not need a timeout. We needed a helicopter rescue.

Despair. Short of unrequited love, it is perhaps the most loathsome of all human emotions. Humiliation would be preferred, for it is fleeting, and from its ashes can arise the hope for another day. Despair is stifling, for it is the stark assertion that hope has passed and that time to come will bring no greater emollient than anguish. C. S. Lewis, in his allegorical masterpiece in the land of Narnia, has his evil White Witch proclaim the fateful words, "despair and die" as she pierces her knife into the languid body of the great lion. Anything else would seem a non sequitur. As it so happened, that was the next play we called in the huddle. "Despair and Die, on Three. Ready. . . . Break."

Norman Maclean, the eminent fishermen, professor, author, student of people (and high school halfback) never published a book until after he turned seventy years old, but spent many years as a writer before that. His most exhausting literary pursuit, short of the sociological forensics surrounding the untimely death of his only brother, was on the subject of failure. He was consumed by the Battle of the Little Bighorn, and more specifically, the famous "last stand" of General George Armstrong Custer, not as a historical event, but as an event whose history gave it breath. He wrote a conglomeration of loosely knit chapters, each one marking its beginning in the days, months, and years after the battle had taken place. What transfixed him as an author searching for resolution were two things: first, that the battle had been placed on such a prominent pillar in the annals of American history after being just one of so many, and having registering just several hundred casualties, but second and more important, that the character of its history is unsure of itself. Are its accents the enshrinement of defeat and failure, or are they perhaps posthumous recompense and tribute to the oppressed Plains Indians? It is true that the defeated people memorialized the battle and its heroes, while neither the Cheyenne nor the Sioux appear to have marked their victory as anything more significant than their continued protestations against inflicted culture. In the end, Maclean abandoned the project because he believed, somewhat ironically, that he himself had failed to offer new humanitarian or scholarly understanding to the ocean swell beneath the history of Custer's Hill, and in literature, failure is not memorialized kindly.

But in his discourse with history, he unearths a rare and enigmatic truth. People, it seems, actually do revel in defeat, as if victory, however elusive, can diminish the luster of life once it has been realized. He quotes George Orwell, whose dark worldview seemingly embraces the ineffable virtues of failure, as evidenced with the blunt remark, "The most stirring battle poem in English is about a brigade of cavalry which charged in the wrong direction." Maclean reminds us, then, "[W]e remember Pearl Harbor, although probably not the name of one of the great battles in which we finally defeated the Japanese." We remember the 1986 World Series for an error at first base, and the fielder and his team are part of baseball legend, but most of us probably don't remember who hit that ball or who scored the winning run on that play . . . or perhaps even who the other team was. We remember the 1993 NCAA men's basketball championship game for a phantom timeout that sealed defeat for the University of Michigan, but most of us probably could not name the victor. In football, when you hear the words "wide right," you think of the Florida State placekicker, but who celebrated these podiatric blunders? And, of course, as long as there are shrines to defeat, there will always be the Chicago Cubs. Our team of football misfits, it would seem, had firmly set the cornerstone for a monumental obelisk that would rise to the clouds exalting our perpetual defeat forevermore.

It is not difficult to articulate the feeling of helplessness, of being overmatched. Simply alluding to it is enough, because each of us has known that feeling, whether in a relationship, a job, a class, a game. What is probably impossible is explaining the way that feeling can be overcome by subconscious resolve, by embers of a spirit snuffed. Perhaps words are not enough to capture the essence of will, just as they are no match for the quandaries and felicity of love. One evening, I had resolved to sit at my desk and work on this transitory passage in this story. I had been passively milling it over for several days in the interstitial recesses that separate original thought from memory, not quite wanting to craft it, but hoping it would emerge. It had stubbornly resisted.

First, though, there was a hockey game to watch. It was the national collegiate Division-I championship game, between Boston University and Miami University of Ohio. Boston University had been the top-ranked team in the nation all year, had won all of its tournaments and accolades, including the exalted Boston Beanpot, and the Hobie Baker award (hockey's Heisman Trophy). The team was packed with professional prospects, had a power play that would have frightened Genghis Khan and his legions, and had won eighteen straight games away from home ice.

With less than a minute remaining in the third and final period, they trailed 3–1. The game and the season were over.

As it happens, Boston University is where I attended college and on whose football field I stood with my band of misplaced brothers so many years ago. Now, on this night, I watched as my alma mater's hockey team remembered who they were and scored two goals in the final sixty seconds of the third period, and another, twelve minutes into overtime. There is my transition.

The hockey team pulled its goalie to yield another offensive skater with almost three minutes remaining in the game, a risky and courageous decision, almost without precedent. Our football team had no goalie to pull, though the idea of one stationed in the end-zone may not have been wholly devoid of merit. But we, too, remembered who we were and from where we had come. There was no championship at stake, no glory, no risk of elimination . . . there was only the season to come and that which had passed, and all the work in between to harden our bodies, and that was enough. Plays began to happen in both directions without the other team scoring, and, for the time, without us scoring either. This was a necessary balance, for not only did it arrest our fatalism, it allowed ample time to regenerate sureness. Had we retaliated quickly on a fluke or errant play, we would have found some measure of satisfaction, but not belief.

As it happened, after several halted drives and exchanges of the ball, we strung several plays together that could best be characterized on their own merits by their mediocrity, but which together moved us steadily downfield. Time neither sped up nor slowed down, as it often does during plays of singular magnificence or monumental underachievement. It simply found a cadence. Within the ineffable triad of virtues that bear success, among talent and trust a good team needs rhythm.

Back to Maclean for a moment, then. The quality of his writing into which he poured the most of his soul was its rhythm. He claimed, "All prose should be rhythmical, (but) one should practically never be consciously aware of the rhythms." Reading any of his narratives or essays or stories without knowing that he said this is the same as reading them *with* the knowledge of his quotation. His rhythms are so subtle as to be imperceptible even when seeking them, and yet their effect creates the intimacy of conversation with the author. Thoughts flow into and out of each other. Tragedy unfolds in a sentence, a paragraph, a story, often abruptly but never surprisingly. The subsurface rhythms and the attendant fluidity of his language lead us into his themes almost by inference.

The game of football is, perhaps, not far removed from good literature if we accept Maclean's maxims and acknowledge that good literature need not be competitive. Probably more than in any other sport, rhythm in football is a gloss that elevates competence to strength. No other sport alternates so immediately and repetitively from full speed to full stop. One way to beat a good team is to impose a rhythm that is unfamiliar, that affords either too much time to overanalyze or not enough time to react. Good players must be instinctive and cerebral in equal measure; keeping a team off its natural or established rhythm destabilizes this balance and allows you to get where they are not, when they are not there.

Duke began drawing up simple plays in the huddle, quickly and deliberately. They were plays we knew would work through the memory in our muscles. They were plays that we could execute quickly, without confusion or extended setup time. They were short yardage plays from which we could regroup rapidly. It was not a hurry-up offense, just a methodical cadence of short simple plays executed in quick enough succession to elude our opponents' ability to react. We got to the places on the field before they did, with just enough time to catch the ball and turn for another yard or two, exactly as Duke had mapped it for us on his shirt. We returned to the huddle, dutifully got our assignments, and did it again and again until we had made it to their fifteen yard line.

Duke drew me up as the primary receiver on the next play, a crossing pattern five yards out in the center of the field. A crossing pattern, a play in which the paths of two receivers cross each other in opposite directions, is designed to confuse the defense momentarily, while the defenders try to avoid each other and decide whether or not to switch their assigned receivers. It is during this brief moment of apprehension, or just afterward, that a short pass can be completed. In this case, the pass would go straight upfield, to me, five yards out, at the moment the receiver from the other side of the field crossed behind me, a little farther downfield. Run correctly, the second receiver can help screen the play without actually interfering with the defense. The risks of the play are that it attracts an inordinate volume of humanity to a single focal point on the field, and collisions and interceptions were not uncommon in our ranks. But we had practiced this a million times.

I lined up in the slot to the left, in between the linemen and another decoy receiver further out, who would draw a defender away from the play down the sideline. On the snap, I took two steps straight downfield and then angled sharply cross-grain toward the center of the field. The play developed quickly enough that I did not have time to make eye contact with my counterpart crossing toward me from the right side of the field. I had to trust that he would run further out and cross behind me so that nobody in the secondary would be between Duke and me. The play does not afford enough time for a defender to gain position between the designated receiver and the quarterback, so if the other receiver coming across ran his route correctly, Duke just had to clear the linemen with the ball and I'd be waiting.

Duke found me with his eyes just before the other receiver crossed behind me and found me with the ball exactly as our two paths crossed, exactly when the defense faced its indecision. I caught the ball and instinctively arced gradually downfield, expecting a defender to emerge from the cluster and strip out my flag since we were all in such close proximity. The play almost always ended right after the catch. It is designed for short yardage, with the expectation that we can clear a path to where they are not, but that they will be there a moment later.

But as I turned my head, and more gradually my body, downfield, I noticed that this time the defense had not yet recovered from its indecision. Apparently, both defenders following the crossing route from two different sides of the field had decided to follow the receiver who crossed behind me. That is to say, one guy switched, and the other guy did not. It happens when instinct and intellect are out of step. This opened an alley for me straight downfield. To my left were now the two defenders recovering from their misdirected momentum, and to my right, well off the play but closing back in now that a ball carrier had materialized, came a third. I simply had to run straight downfield another ten yards and beat them all to the endzone before they closed. I could tell that I had the first two guys beat. They had no angle on me and no momentum. The third defender, closing along the goal line from the right, did have an angle and was coming hard. I had no blockers since the play was not supposed to ever get this far.

Wheeling a football downfield is an exhilarating experience, even for people like me who are not particularly fleet of foot. You become the center of attention, the sole target of malice, and moments like this either accentuate your inadequacies or your abilities to overcome them. Trained athletes can run fast by thinking about it, but mere mortals have to propel ourselves with something more innate. The cerebral encumbrances of *trying* to run fast will usually slow you down, but *needing* to get somewhere safe quickly can tap into some surprising propulsive reserves. The difference between trying to be fast and needing to be fast is not as subtle as it might seem, but understanding it can have a profound impact on athletic prowess. When my son turned six years old, he tried on his first pair of baseball pants and cleated shoes. I inquired about the fit. "How does everything feel?" I asked. "Dad," he said before even taking a step, "I feel fast." As I turned upfield against that divided defense in the middle of the field along the crest of the arched and unyielding Astroturf, I felt it too. For the first time in my life, I felt it simply because I needed it. I had in front of me a ten-yard carnivorous scramble. So I ran.

I ran fast enough that it actually required an effort to decelerate, and I did not stop until I had passed straight through the endzone and off the field. I glanced downward to make sure that nobody had stripped my flag from my waist, and to my wonder, the stadium lights surrounding the south endzone gave proof through that night that my flag was still there. Touchdown. It was the first touchdown

I had ever scored in an official football game, which is to say a game that is sanctioned by a higher authority and whose results are recorded by somebody other than the players. I admit that I was distracted by this personal realization, but only for a moment. This game was now a contest.

And so it remained, well into the second half. After giving up two touchdowns on the first two plays from scrimmage, we had either found a defensive rhythm or had matched their offensive rhythm—it is often hard to tell who is leading the dance. We still trailed two touchdowns to one, or twelve to six. Extra points in this league were the equivalent of two-point conversion plays in higher levels of the game, though only one point was awarded. The point would be secured upon the completion of a passing play into the endzone from the three yard line following a touchdown. In this game, neither team had managed to convert any of the extra point opportunities into points. The score was twelve to six.

Then, midway through the second half, we found ourselves on the five yard line, poised to tie the game. In the huddle, Duke called the same play as the one that had secured our first score. Crossing pattern across the middle. I lined up in the same slot, took my two steps, cut across the field, and caught the ball. And a strange thing happened.

Two yards still separated me from the goal line, but I slowed down even before turning my head or my body. I did not so much turn and scramble as I simply arced toward the endzone without earnest. This was not arrogance. I did not walk or strut into the endzone. It was quiet confidence, aroused by knowledge that the play had worked even before it was complete, and that we had tied the game even before we had tied the game. It was instinct, but more than that, it was grace. My forty years as a starving athlete can most easily be described with allusions to three-legged camels or a drunken ox, but for one singular moment, I felt graceful. To describe such an ephemeral feeling would, in a way, disgrace it. The only comparable experiences have come on the basketball court, when the outcome of a play reveals itself even before it happens, and the surety of success becomes fluidity and nobody can stop a flowing river. I drifted three or four strides into the endzone, arcing toward it effortlessly, skating instead of running. Tie game.

It was powerfully tempting to call the same play for the extra point. It had completely flummoxed our opponents twice, and they had no idea how to defend it. But we also figured that they would probably be expecting it and planning more cerebrally this time, so Duke drew up a completely new play on the spot, one that we had never tried, and one that could possibly establish our credibility as players in a league of players by putting us in the lead.

We lined up, our whole team facing straight ahead toward the arcing dormitories that had once been our window into this proving ground. It was time to determine if we had a right to be there.

Down. . . .

Set. . . .

Hike. . . . Hike!

Duke took the snap and immediately rolled hard to his left. As if they were tethered, the line shifted with him, step for step. All four receivers, two from the left and two from the right, ran slant patterns to the left of the field. Everybody was running toward the back left corner of the endzone, and naturally, the defense followed, just as it had followed my father as he had pulled to the right on his first play.

Then Duke stopped abruptly and planted his right foot, pivoting on it so that his body now faced the lonely morass which was the right side of the field. One or two seconds earlier, one of our receivers who had lined up on the right and had streaked left with everybody else had slowed down and drifted back to the right nonchalantly, eyes averting the entire play, as if he did not understand it. His confused demeanor and position were so conspicuous as to be nearly invisible and wholly unthreatening. Nobody in the secondary paid him an ounce of attention. He was an engineering student playing like an engineering student, that was all. In a sense, they were right. Of all the diagrams we drew of forces and acceleration and momentum, this was easily the most elegant. It was the easiest pass Duke ever made, like playing catch. On a play originating from the three yard line, the receiver caught the ball without anybody else on the field within twenty yards of him. Thirteen to twelve, our lead.

That is all I remember from this game, as the supporting details about drives and sustaining plays have naturally faded with time. But the plays in the game that yielded points remain viscerally clear in my memory. They were the only five plays in the game that yielded any points; two touchdowns for each team, and an extra point for us. I do not recall what adjustments we made to hold our opponents scoreless for an entire game minus the first two plays. I do remember the paradoxical feeling that accompanied us off the field and which replaced relief with the gravity of expectation bequeathed upon those who belong. We all look fondly upon the lives of our heroes, and wonder at their sober, even somber view of their world. Why do they not smile more often? Would that they could with the weight of responsibility upon their being. We smiled, a bit, in tempered doses. We belonged there, and now had to stay.

And, as I do not recall many of the individual plays that supported our victory that evening, neither do I remember many details among the handful of games that comprised the rest of our season. We ran our exalted out and up pattern with great success, though it was negated more than once by false start penalties. Our short yardage crossing patterns became our mainstay, and our defense was disciplined because we had drilled ourselves in the passive aggressiveness of man-to-man coverage back at the caged field. We did not win every game, but neither did we lose many. We won enough games to belong on that field, underneath the lights, surrounded by the dormitories and those who now looked down longingly from on high, at us. It was all we had wanted.

And so we found ourselves later that autumn in the playoffs, a five-round, single-elimination tournament structured like the annual NCAA basketball tournament, but with thirty-two teams instead of sixty-four. The eventual champion would have to win five straight games against progressively better opponents. Our season record had earned us a seeding in the middle of the pack of thirty-two teams, teams with guys who had played real football in high school, teams that had beaten us thirty-five to nothing the previous year. None of us allowed ourselves to think that we could win it all, but all of us knew that we could win a game on any day. We knew that this would probably be our last run together as a team. Many of us would be seniors the following year and the academic schedule, like a good tournament, promised to amplify its intensity. Others, naturally, would leave college early for the draft. This was our run for the roses, or the petunias, or the dandelions . . . however far we could get before our final "off-season," a term we felt privileged now to use, because this year it would be discernable from the season itself.

Eventually, our run would culminate in a single play, as great tournaments so often do. Athletic tournaments, especially those in which a single loss leads to elimination, are adrenaline dam breaks. Nothing I know matches the focused intensity, the peril perceived, and the awkward imbalance of self-assuredness and complete uncertainty (well, almost nothing).

Flipping channels one late night years ago, I stumbled across a televangelist crooning with a variety of bloated platitudes until he at last asked a question which startled me at first and troubled me for quite some time afterwards. "How," he asked, "how can this be? You good people can fill this football stadium tonight and clap politely when I tell you that eternal salvation is yours, and you same good people will fill this same stadium tomorrow and blow the roof off when your team scores six points! How can this be? Why aren't you pumping your fists in the air now, tonight? Why are you clapping and not leaping and dancing? Why are six points more important to you people than eternal life? Why?"

Having been raised in a more subdued Protestant home, I found this question troubling. Our family church, as a body, was not one to stake any claim on exuberance. Our weekly services were more catechism than revival, influenced more by John Calvin than by John Madden. My faith has liberalized somewhat in adulthood, but has always remained intact at its roots, meaning that while its revelations have evolved, neither its tenets nor its demeanor have changed much. And so I wondered why, when comparing Dante Culpepper with Dante's *Inferno*, the former naturally evokes so much more emotion. I admit that I have never found the words of televangelists to be particularly compelling, but these, indeed, required some reckoning.

When profound questions reveal their truths, they relinquish their original depth and become simple, often wholesome, observations. What if the crowd knew the score before the game? And what if, just one night earlier, the eternal fate of the crowd had been determined by the flip of a coin? "Ok flock, heads it's everlasting peace, tails it's eternal suffering and misery.[1] " I would confidently suggest that a favorable coin toss would have elicited the baring of soul and spirit that would make any touchdown celebration seem like an algebra test. The intensity, the adrenaline, come from not knowing what is about to happen. Good news is at its best, by far, the moment it is revealed.

What good news awaited us? Was there any?

Our opening round game, played under the lights, set us against a team with an odd assortment of players. Some of the guys, the big ones, I knew from the basketball courts. Good guys, good players. They had played in high school with helmets and pads instead of the little nylon garlands draped loosely around our waist waiting to be "tackled." The team also sported a short, awkward looking player, quite familiar to us in both physique and social graces. We immediately recognized him as a converted referee, he of the ilk that castigated and ejected me the previous year for the use of sarcasm during a football game. We did not know his name, but we had plenty of worthy substitutes.

"This can't be good," I mumbled to Duke as we took the field.

---

1. In sports parlance, this question can be easily rephrased: "Heads and you are champions, tails and you are Cubs fans."

"Mmmmm. Nope."

"Better hold our tongues. I hear they are cracking down this year on alliteration and split infinitives."

But, try as we might to avoid the filing of grievances, we failed. The game was tough and close from start to finish, and with time left at the end for just one play, we found ourselves inside our opponents' five yard line, trailing by less than a touchdown (by virtue of some odd assortment of failure and success on the extra points throughout the game). Last play—if we scored, we advanced to the second round. If they stopped us, our season and our reconciliation were over, prematurely by our reckoning. Duke drafted the play on his shirt.

I lined up in the slot to the left, my frequent assignment, but as a decoy. This play was to the right. I had drawn their tallest defender all through the game, and that left the right side marginally vulnerable.

Ready.

Set.

Hike! Hike! Hike!

I angled for the back left of the endzone to draw my defender away from the play. Duke slung a quick drop pass to the receiver in the right slot, who then propelled himself forward toward the goal line. Defenders converged, it was still anybody's game to win.

You may recall John Elway's famous head-first dive that helped the Denver Broncos preserve a crucial drive inside the five yard line and win their first Super Bowl in 1997. It has become as iconic as any of his late game comeback drives for which he is so deservedly revered. At considerable risk to his future ambulation, he lifted off and, by all visual accounts, worried not at all about how or where or in what position he might re-enter the playing field until after he had been pinwheeled by two closing Green Bay Packers. It was as courageous a play as you will ever see a quarterback make, and the ballistics were spectacular. It was the kind of play that foreshadows victory, long after the era in which foreshadowing was frequently flagged as a fifteen-yard penalty.

Our own play occurred well before John Elway made his famous leap, and though one of our receivers bore a striking physical resemblance to the real athlete, he was not the ball carrier on this play. Our man who was carrying the ball leaned toward the goal line as he ran, then just before crossing it, he vaulted himself between the encroaching defenders, head first, and twisting his body as if it were a torpedo, making it that much more difficult to grab his flags for the tackle. He landed in the endzone, flags intact, rose gallantly from the turf, and the game was over. We had won.

We shook hands with our opponents, careful to enunciate "good game" very clearly to avoid any ambiguity or misconstructions of our intended phrasing. In many ways, our season was complete, even though the playoffs had just begun. We had proven that we could post a respectable record through the season, and we had now advanced in the playoffs, a considerable accomplishment in any sport at any level because of the attendant intensity. The victory had been an unthinkable accomplishment just twelve months earlier. And, with just a spritz of poetry, we had beaten the team with the retired referee who used literary devices against our team of technocrats.

Aye, there's the rub. He would not go gentle into that good night. The next morning, as Duke and I were milling about our apartment preparing for classes, the telephone rang. Duke answered.

"Your dime." It was his customary greeting, always delivered with a charming inflection that conveyed his implied wink.

". . ."

"What do you mean?"

". . ."

"You gotta be kidding me. Can they do that?"

". . ."

"Yeah, well, I guess maybe he did, but nobody called any penalty. . . ."

". . ."

"When?"

". . ."

"Tonight? You gotta . . . you gotta be kiddin' me. C'mon, I can't get a whole team together with one day's notice."

". . ."

"What?!"

". . ."

"Right, yeah, thanks a lot." This time without a wink, and with a charm much more sour than before.

It seems, quite reasonably in retrospect, that our league had a rule that strictly forbade diving. Naturally, this is to protect all of the combatants, unclad as we were with any protective gear. It was a good rule, but one with which the referees of the previous evening were wholly unfamiliar. They had not flagged the play. They had ruled touchdown. There was no instant replay back then.

But our friend, the one-time referee, knew all of the rules in the book, and a few more that he invented as circumstances warranted. He had filed a protest with the commissioner (who that was for an intramural flag football league I have no idea), and, according to the league rules that he knew so well, the only way to resolve a protest in a single-elimination playoff tournament if the complaint was legitimate (which it was, and which we did not contest) was to replay. Not the entire game, just everything from the point of the infraction. That is, we had to show up to repeat the final play of the game. If we failed to field a full team that night, just a few hours away, we would forfeit our victory. If we failed to score, likewise. It is not unusual to have an entire season depend on a single play. What *is* unusual is to know well ahead of time that your season will depend on just one play and to have lots of time to think about it. There would be many integrals and second derivatives left un-solved on this day.

The complaint, we realized, was justified. The resolution was just. We had scored the winning points with an illegal play. Had it been flagged when it occurred, we would have lost the game. Nei-ther was the complaint petty. The rule is quite reasonable and was instituted to protect the well-being of the players. What bothered us was that our situation was preposterous, and the perpetrator knew it. There was no way that we could rustle up a complete team with just a few hours of notice. College students have busy academic and social schedules, and we weren't sure which *Star Trek* episode might be on that night. We suspected that the plaintiff had re-quested an accelerated resolution through his contacts in the league's "front office." We could have inquired as to whether his complaint had been filed with any dangling participles, but that may not have helped our cause a great deal.

As I said before, engineers as a breed usually do not accept failure without questioning its precursors and altering them. "I don't think they liked losing to a bunch of gangly engineers," we chortled amongst ourselves. "Hmmm. Imagine how they might feel if they lost twice." Our situation drew some quick attention, and all of our players eagerly signed on for an encore of the final play, in altered form. How many times in the history of sports has the last play of an elimination game, or any game, been played twice on successive evenings? *Star Trek* could wait. And in tribute to the academic predilections of the plaintiff, I offer this borrowed account:

Once upon an evening dreary, while we pondered, worn and weary,
Over curious and dishonorable annulment of the score,
We'd arisen from quaint slumber to behold diminished number
Of the total points encumbered on our foes the eve before.
Furrowed brows adorned the victors, for the vanquished did implore,
"Rise again, and score once more."

Ah, distinctly I recall the mournful omen of that fall,
In that telephonic message and the fate it held in store.
Loathesome, then, upon the morrow while in vainly muffled sorrow,
Did we thus attempt to borrow some mystique from local lore,
From the legends of finale, Flutie, Fisk, and Bobby Orr,
Here enshrined forevermore.

Presently our souls grew stronger, hesitating then no longer,
Strode we out to reacquaint with those we'd conquered hours afore.
Though oppressive lights demanding our deserved reprimanding,
The opponents 'fore us standing were not those we'd met before,
Not in distant times nor since the chimes had counted twenty-four,
Never once in days of yore.

Diminution of our glory seemed our fateful course of story,
For the foes before us standing were much larger than before.
Though destitute of reason to commit the likes of treason,
'Gainst the sport and, too, our season, the same uniforms they wore,
As the foes who vanquished grumbled at their fate the night before,
Vanished now forevermore.

And so to us it was revealed, the frail motive once concealed,
These behemoth mercenaries were but hired to restore

Honor to the most deserving, and with presence most unnerving,
O'er the turf so gently curving sought they justice in the score.
Bitterly our souls grew weary, such foul play did we deplore,
Though we could do nothing more.

So the field where once, as tenants, we had gazed now asked for penance
Not just for the way as victors we had reigned the eve before,
Aye, the iron bells now tolling did reproach without extolling,
The trespass of high hope strolling through as yet unwritten lore.
Such ephemeral redemption naught but torments! Grasp it or,
Banished be forevermore!

Pallid then we took our places 'gainst the stony bulwark faces,
Which adorned each earnest yeoman of the foes who played no more.
Stood we faint on ground once hallowed, now of triumph fully fallowed
Trembled we, as on the gallows, tempests rising from our core,
Would we seal our fate of folly or reprise one night of yore?
It was now, or nevermore.

Suddenly there came a tapping and a flurry and a flapping,
As some darkened gothic creature cloaked in night above did soar.
'Twas a raven who'd mistaken this quaint poem I've forsaken
As the real one, not one taken from its rightful author's lore,
And its countenance with terror knew its error as it swore,
"Curséd be, you will not score!"

Had we wrought not ample anguish, were our souls condemned
        to languish
In the shadow of this demon fowl whose wings foul portent bore?
Our condition was absurd enough without this phantom bird,
And in vain we sought the word we knew would banish it once more,
To its musty tattered pages, to some perch above a door,
Yet we found it nevermore.

Aye, but had we some discretion to establish vague impression
Of our literary forebears 'midst our stern curricular core,
Might we then have fain remembered, lest we soon would

be dismembered,
That elusive word whose embers did our ignorance implore,
But entombed in mathematics did our consciousness ignore,
Famous words like "Nevermore."

Had that word by us been uttered surely then he may have stuttered,
That dark raven who entreated now our foes to bar the door.
Yet it hovered o'er the ball casting malefactor's pall
Mocking pedigree and all its arduous honor we'd fought for,
Which just now upon the threshold of our fate we might restore,
Failing that, then Nevermore.

"Curse thee, dark malicious raven! Seek we now our righteous haven,
O'er that yonder line beyond you just three yards, or maybe four."
And our man the ball did carry, neither wan nor was he wary
Destined not to moil nor tarry did he stage our grand encore.
Neither prostrate nor recumbent but upright now did he score.
Victors we, forevermore.

Birds of all feathers have found their way into sporting lore. Most of us have seen the seagull on the seventeenth green fly away with Steve Lowery's golf ball before dropping it into the drink. So, too, have we seen the burst of feathers which had been a wayward fowl until the moment it met a ninety-eight mile-per-hour Randy Johnson fastball broadside. And more recently the mascot of the Atlanta Hawks, a live hawk, decided to perch not atop a chamber door, but atop the shot clock, which is decidedly less ominous, but also more obtrusive. I wonder what it quothed while perched up there. And, as I write I am but one night removed from a flock of seagulls in Cleveland who, at no little expense to one of their number, redirected a base hit away from the awaiting center fielder in the bottom of the ninth inning, allowing the Indians to score the winning run.[2] But to my knowledge, this is the first account of a raven interfering in modern competition, and raises an ungainly prospect that as a species, its days of yore may have been less saintly than once imagined.

Admittedly, this has been an ornamental retelling.[3] The journalistic version simply had us running the same play we had successfully run the night before. How would they recognize it? None of the new opponents had been there to see it the first time, save our friend who had filed the grievance. We worried little about him, as his defensive skills matched our dexterity in Latin conjugation. Our man sprinted into the endzone, handed the ball politely to the referee, we shook hands with our new opponents, again, and went home. We had won this game twice.

And as it is in any single-elimination tournament (using the term loosely here, since we had singly eliminated our opponent twice), the spoils of our campaign were the right to extend it further. The previous year, any onlooker would have tried in vain to distinguish our foiled faces from the field itself, as both presented equal measures of flesh and turf. Now, we stood among the half of the teams still standing. Poe would have been proud, especially if he had foreseen that his ghastly bird would become the namesake of the modern day football team in the city he called home:

> Perched that raven e'er eternal o'er the door with gaze infernal
> Yet his form is not confined to hallowed literary lore,
> For as restless Colts took leave of their fair city, left to grieve,

---

2. Perhaps the first ever "flock-off" hit in the history of major league baseball, if I may.

3. Ornamental, perhaps, but grammatically flawed (a fifteen-yard infraction). Can you find the dangling modifier?

A faithful lot did fain believe a team would rise again once more,
To reclaim the city's honor on the cold Atlantic shore,
Ravens, hence, of Baltimore.

We cannot hold memory accountable for each footfall of a sustained march. I can recall only two salient facts about our second-round game in this five-round tournament. I cannot recall the opponent, nor the final score. It might have been close, or it might have been lopsided. The first of the two facts is this: if reminiscence of our first-round game calls to mind an image of the stately raven, our second-round game casts an ungainly shadow through time of a wounded duck with cramps. Frequently, a hapless forward pass in which the ball rotates conspicuously on more than one axis, tumbles really, elicits catcalls from friends and foes alike, hailing the gracefulness of the ball's aching flight as that of an immobilized mallard after a direct hit. But Duke threw no ducks. His passes were always crisp and tight. No, it was me. I, myself, was the duck.

You may recall that the reason Duke frequently looked first to me when choosing a receiver was that I never broke form, never once ran a pass pattern contrary to the way it was wired in his mind. Five steps and in was five steps and in, not six. Ten yards and out was ten yards and straight out, no angle. When you know with absolute certainty where your teammates will be, you are one step ahead of the play itself and can plainly visualize what happens before it happens, because you know it will happen. Whether by foreknowledge of a teammate's ability to arrive or of your own ability to deliver, this preordained certainty is perhaps the single greatest competitive advantage in any sport. Thinking takes time. Knowing does not. Those hundredths of seconds make a difference.

Early in the game, I was given my assignment in the huddle. Line up wide to the left, go five yards out, and cut straight across the middle. Simple play, we ran it all the time for short yardage. We were at midfield and hoping to sustain a drive in our usual way. I lined up wide to the left, the only receiver on my side of the field. The defense was playing single coverage across the field, which meant that they had assigned only one defender to my side of the field, to guard me. And for reasons I cannot explain, he did not line up opposite my position. Rather, he hedged toward the center of the field by at least seven or eight yards. Either he recognized the play we were running, or, more likely, he was not paying close attention. If he had examined our relative positions as he should have, he would have realized what I had quickly realized. I had half a football field all to myself. . . .

But it was not the half into which I was assigned to run. All young men ambling through the interminable void between adolescence and young adulthood face moral trials that amply determine how gracefully they might enter life's next phase. My life was no different. My trials up to that point had their origins in teenage vice: alcohol, girls, and practical jokes. I managed to avoid the first two almost entirely, though not necessarily out of a sense of moral rectitude. But generally, when facing life-altering choices, my morals earned their laurels. I cannot claim such respectability when trying to avoid the allure of a good joke at someone else's expense. Whether setting up trip wires in my house or strafing late-night club goers with water balloons from above, a good joke to me has always been irresistible. It is a character flaw that forever marks me as happily undignified, but I would wager that the attendant hilarity has added years to my life.

As I stood all alone on the left side of the field that afternoon, I found myself at the precipice of moral decay. Breaking a pattern would betray a trust that had never been broken and might never again be regained. I took this far more seriously than perhaps I should have, but I also credit my literalist approach to the game as one feather in our cap of success. This was no practical joke to me. The Astroturf was now moral ground which offered two paths: one to honor, the other to glory. I had this much time to make my decision.

As soon as the ball was in play, I broke form and ran for glory. Instead of running straight ahead and turning toward the center of the field, I angled straight toward the sideline, away from everybody and completely unattended by any defender. I raised my hand and called Duke's name as loud as I could, because I knew that he would be looking for me right then at the middle of the field. He saw me and instantly recognized that we had capitalized on a defensive oversight. It is called "reading the defense," and good teams will scour the defensive setup and make adjustments in the play, sometimes verbally, sometimes telepathically. It is just usually not this easy. He slung the ball to me, I stuttered my steps to catch it because our improvised timing was not perfect, and turned upfield right along the sideline for a twenty-yard jog into the endzone. The defender had not even followed me. I could have walked and scored easily, but that would have been impolite, and I hoped to retain whatever dignity remained after so brazenly forsaking all that is good and true.

And then I tripped.

By this, I do not mean to say that I stumbled momentarily. My vestibular system cross-wired and my equilibrium took its leave. I plummeted headlong toward the turf, not knowing what had caused this disintegration of the glorious play, nor what I could do to arrest the fall. Instinctively, my hand reached out and landed awkwardly on the turf an instant before my knees settled in behind it, which would have been the end of the play. Still, I lunged. I had behind me, if not my own inertia, certainly that of an overachieving team, and I could not stop moving. Neither could I restore myself to an upright position. What I knew was that I must keep moving forward as best I could, hand over foot, and that I must not let my knees scrape the turf. Quothed the duck, "I have to score!"

Instinctively, again, I raised my hind quarters as high into the air as possible in the subliminal hope that my knees would follow. This created the ungainly impression of a rolling triangle. My body bent in half at its apex, my waist, as my legs angled behind trying to catch up with my free hand that was, of its own accord, angling forward toward the ground and galloping quite freely, it being the only ambulatory alternative to my face.

I never spoke to anybody on my team about this play after the game. I never asked what they were thinking as they watched or for solace that my appearance was not as bad as it felt. But I imagine that they looked on and mused to themselves that this was how it would all end. After all our self-imposed toughening and discipline, after our comebacks, reprises, and reprisals, our chance for an open touchdown and the lead in a playoff game would end in our receiver tripping over himself and falling.

Worse, the defender who had paid me as much attention as he might a falling leaf, now charged toward what he must have perceived as a break-dancing camel stumbling down the sideline. Twenty yards . . . this is embarrassing. . . . Fifteen yards . . . he is closing. . . . Ten yards . . . hold the ball tight. . . . Five yards . . . this hurts as much as it looks like it does . . . wait now, touchdown!

I think he had been with me for the last few steps, but trying to disengage the flags around my waist would have been harder than grabbing one particular sock out of the spin cycle. We had scored a touchdown by reading the defense and adjusting, a facet of our game heretofore unthinkable, clearly reserved for teams at a higher level, and apparently with good reason. Six points were our generous reward. The specter of the least nimble conflagration of arms and legs one might ever see became my lasting reproach. I have never again broken form.[4]

At the outset of my reminiscence of this game, I noted that I recalled two facts, and so far I have noted but one. The second is that in the end, we won the game. In football, points are neither awarded nor deducted for artistic impression. My sideline conniption was worth the same amount of points as Dwight Clark's Superbowl catch, Boise State's statue of liberty, and Gerard Phelan's miraculous reception. It was enough to help us win the game, and now, three out of every four teams had been eliminated . . . but we were still playing. One more win and we would be in the final four, playing with guys who had not only played high school football, but who had no doubt also won district and state championships along the way, who knew what a counter trap was, who routinely

---

4.   As if needing a reprise of our first round victory were not enough, several nights after I wrote the reminiscence of my sideline floundering in our second playoff game, my prominent imbalance returned. I was trying to score from second base on a line drive in a softball game. The play was going to be close, but the game was tied and it was an even bet. Halfway to the plate, my neurons took their leave and I momentarily lost all sensation in my legs. I stumbled, staggered, and finally collapsed face first in the dirt . . . five feet shy of the plate. The catcher walked over and tagged me out while I lay prostrate and motionless. My whole right forearm was a bleeding mess—that must be where I "landed." I reminded my teammates that Jacoby Ellsbury of the Red Sox stumbled badly when he stole home earlier in the year against the Yankee's Andy Pettite. They reminded me that he covered the full distance and was safe. Anyway, we won 19–3 after my baserunning disaster loosened our spirits. I should probably be checked out by somebody, but who?

read the defense and adjusted without losing their senses, and who could not care less what we or anybody else quothed.

On the Saturday afternoon of the third playoff game, about half of our team gathered at the entrance of our apartment building. A narrow driveway ran between two identical buildings, emptying into two separate streets on either end. Across one street was the twelve-foot chain-link fence, always encircling our hopeful practice field, which was quiet on this day. The other street wound gently through a quiet neighborhood of single family and duplex apartments, and eventually, right to the football stadium.

We often walked on the street itself, as we did on this day. Most of the residents relied on the nearby trolley to move throughout the city, and moving cars were infrequent here. Sometimes we would play catch along the way, and sometimes we would just walk and talk, calmly preparing. Parked cars on the street were infrequent, too. Most were nestled into impossibly small driveways overgrown with foliage contrived to afford small doses of privacy from the residence next door. But on this day, there was a car parked in the street, about twenty yards ahead of us as we walked.

"Hey Kirk, run up to that car at full speed. Don't look back until you get there, and then look over your right shoulder. The ball will be right there." It was Duke's suggestion, a carefree challenge to our metaphysical connection.

Ever obedient to my quarterback, I bolted down the street, reached the car, turned inward to the right, and grabbed the football out of the air. It was right there.

"Not bad," I called. "Can you do it again?" I tossed the ball back. "No parked car this time, though. No landmark. I'm going the same distance."

"You got it," was Duke's reply. Without a landmark, this was surely a fuller test of our attunement. How well did he know where I would be and what I would be thinking? How well did I know he knew these things?

I ran about twenty yards, in my estimation, and turned slightly inward, looking back over my shoulder. The ball was right there.

"Again."

"You got it."

The ball was right there. We continued until we came to Commonwealth Avenue and our quiet residential neighborhood yielded to the city. Here ended the frivolity, for pass plays on Commonwealth Avenue usually end badly. But on the way, we had never missed once. It is called a timing pattern, a play designed to blend deception with precision, and safety with risk. We had just run the play as a way to synchronize our minds with our hands, and with each other's minds. Real players run the play to let the quarterback release the ball as soon as possible, and to avoid identifying the intended receiver to a defender until the last possible second, when the receiver finally turns and the ball is right there. When the play is run well, a man-to-man defender is watching the receiver and not the quarterback and will not have time to move toward the ball until it is too late. The play is often run toward the sidelines, so that the safeties, the last line of defense and those whose eyes should be on the quarterback while their legs follow the receivers, cannot close the distance once the ball is in flight. The quarterback takes just a few steps back and heaves the ball into a high arc so that it remains aloft long enough for his receiver to drift underneath it to the point of rendezvous. It is perhaps one of football's safest plays at its outset because the quarterback lofts the ball immediately and cannot be sacked. After that, it is perhaps the game's most risky play because the pass is in the air on its way to a preordained receiver long before anybody knows how well he might be covered. A good quarterback can throw the ball so that its only two physically possible landing zones will be the receiver's hands or out of bounds, but still, it is a play of inescapable destiny.

In our case, it was a good way to warm up, a good way to synchronize our minds and muscles with each other's. We had never run the play before. In games at our level, with three or four prospective receivers on any given play running patterns against unprepared defenses, it made little sense to commit to any one possibility before knowing how open he, or the others, might be.

Across Commonwealth Avenue and just past a formidable brick armory building was the entrance to the stadium, and through that, the broad steps that slanted toward the field. The turf was bright green in the midday sun, luminous enough to forebode against trespassing. Perhaps not as pastoral, but as profound as William Blake's echoing green of games past, it stretched before us awaiting a game today. Time had come to wake up the echoes and shake down some thunder. We hoped that the echoes were the right ones, and that the thunder blew in with a favoring wind.

The opposing team assembled on the opposite side of the echoing green. If we were the echoes, they were the thunder. To a man, they were more athletic than we were. But, so too were most of the men on the other teams we had played, and whom we had beaten. You can feel superior and not win, but you cannot feel inferior and not lose.

We ran our proven offense, reliable and only sometimes flashy. We ran crossing patterns. We ran our out-and-ups. We did not run any counter traps. We ran fades and posts. We never read the defense. We never broke form. The echoes were not long distant. The rhythm of the season was unbroken.

They ran a tough offense, fast and strong and clean.

Both teams played defense like the cliffs of Dover against the sea, and kept the thunder at a safe distance. Only once in the first half did a player cross the goal line with the ball in hand. Well, twice actually. We scored the extra point that accompanied the game's solitary touchdown. At halftime, we led seven to nothing.

Our opponents were flummoxed, and they clearly regarded our modest lead as an encroachment against eternal truths that segregate human beings by their physical virtues. Were not the Greek gods themselves the forebears of the Olympic games by virtue of their great mountain resort? I dare say that no supernatural beings inspired the SATs. All they did for us was give us honoraria like *magna cum laude* . . . or was that Latin? Either way, no *cum laude* in any of its exalted manifestations ever landed anybody a signing bonus. Sir Isaac Newton may have unraveled gravitational mysteries and invented calculus, but he never had his face on a bubble gum trading card. David slew Goliath with a stone and was anointed king, but I would wager that he had to take his SATs more than once to crack six hundred. In our world, as in those past, virility has been demonstrated by feats of strength, endurance, speed, and precision. While almost anybody off the street would tell you that these are precisely the qualities that allow one to calculate thermonuclear reaction rates or subsurface wave propagation, we must agree that society at large recognizes the most distinguished accomplishments of its members as those achieved with muscles and organs below the neck . . . all of them. Our spindly legs and numerical predilections still stood on this day as a bold, if somewhat uncertain challenge to this tradition that has, as best as I can tell, spanned all of human and supernatural history.

This truth was not lost on our opponents. Long before the New England Patriots were caught stealing defensive signals from their opponents, our band of brothers unwittingly foreshadowed the scandal with a bit of accidental espionage.[5] One of our truest friends, our solitary fan throughout the season who never missed a game, walked past our opponents during their halftime break while on her way to get a drink of water. As she passed them, she overheard the echoes of Greek gods, wondering how it could be that mere mortals were now overtaking them. "How can *we* be losing to *them*?" The essence of the question was in its inflection. They were not seeking a revised game plan, nor questioning their own ability. They were questioning the great truths of evolution, ascension, and football. How could the hare lose to the tortoise? How could the Philistines retreat from a boy? How could Oklahoma lose to Boise State in a bowl game? How could anybody lose to the Patriots in a Super Bowl? How can this be?

We received this bit of reconnaissance with more than a bit of glee. Deceptive noodleness paired with methodical precision crafts a formidable team because of the obvious contradictions and maddening persistence in the opposing psyche. The question of how *we* could be losing to *them* was rhetorical, of course. It was Zeus and Apollo venting their frustration. Nevertheless, we had an answer and so did they. Our answer was very pragmatic, and could be found within the confines of the fenced-in grassy enclave where we

---

5.   Bill Belichick, coach of the New England Patriots, was fined half a million dollars for his role in the scandal. Imagine what the penalty might have been if the charge of foreshadowing had also been levied against him.

had met each Sunday. It seems, though, that whatever their answer was, it was more compelling.

Thinking back now on that question of frustration, I can see how it could have also been powerfully persuasive to anyone belonging to the *we*. As halftime speeches go, it has to rank among the most concise, and perhaps the most profound. And because of that, it resonated among the *we*. Early in the second half, they (the *we*) scored a touchdown and came within a point of tying the game. But our defense held firm and prevented the extra point, so we led seven to six. Their defense, too, held its ground with newfound resolve, and we exhausted our entire repertoire of plays without sustaining a successful drive.

Midway through the second half, we still held a one point advantage, but it was quickly subdued by our opponents' quest to restore truth, justice, and reduced entropy to the universe. They scored another touchdown and now led the game twelve to seven. An extra point would put them ahead by a full touchdown, and we would have to win by a touchdown and an extra point at a point in the game when neither our long routes nor our short patterns were at all effective. If they failed to score the extra point, we had a chance of getting lucky on just one play . . . equally the most engaging and cathartic situation in any sport because everybody knows that it *could* happen in an instant, but that it almost certainly *will not*. If you know what I'm talking about, you can hear the telecaster's call weaving in and out of this paragraph: "The winning run steps to the plate." "This bunker shot would win the cup." "Eight-tenths of a second on the clock for the inbound pass—two to tie, three to win." "Flutie flushed . . . throws it down. . . ."

Their extra point pass fell harmlessly to the turf. Twelve to seven. One play is all we needed.

But none of our plays were working. They had figured them out and knew how to defend us. And suddenly, we found ourselves at the end, holding the ball for what we knew would be the final drive of the game. Twelve to seven. Just one play could do it. And we moved, slowly, as they assumed a more conservative defensive posture, guarding against that one play that would span the field (a posture normally referred to in regretful elegies as a "prevent defense"). The green turf opened up in patches close by, and we caught short passes for short gains until finally we had reached their twenty yard line, with time for just one more play. We ambled into the huddle exhausted and unsure. A short play would do nothing for us now. And though it would be poetic, we were too close to the endzone for a Hail Mary. We needed an elegant and ingenious idea.

Duke did not draw anything on his shirt. He looked me in the eyes and said confidently, "Kirk, the play from the street. It's the only thing we haven't tried, and it's the same distance. Line up in the left slot. Break hard off the line of scrimmage. Shoot straight downfield, eyes forward. After you cross the line, curl inward just enough to look back over your right shoulder. The ball will be right there."

Everyone nodded in agreement, full of ambivalence and confidence in equal measure and having no better ideas to offer. Duke drew up assignments for all the other receivers, but we knew that these were decoys. The ball would be in flight in another direction before they were four steps off the line. Our season came down to an untested play that would rest upon the metaphysical connection between two guys who were roommates, friends, and teammates.

I lined up wide to the left and looked downfield toward the goal line, once again facing the arcing façades of the surrounding dormitories. Our game, our season, on our field. That line, twenty yards distant, is where I would turn my head, and the ball would be right there. That's how we drew it up. There were no alternate receivers on this play. It was coming to me no matter how well I might be covered. No option. All or nothing. We either win or lose, right now.

In the street on the way to the game, it had worked every time, but we had never run the play against an opposing defense. If the receiver turns his head too early and makes even slight adjustments to the ball with his body or eyes, the defender is tipped off that his man is the true target and he closes in. My job was to get behind the defender and separate enough from him to create a pocket for the ball, which would be on its way as all of this was happening. This had to happen in the twenty yards between the goal line and me, because when I reached the line, I had to turn around. But en route, I had to let the defender think that I might be just a decoy until the very moment I caught the ball. He had to cover me *and* the rest of the team, to some degree.

I broke hard off the line of scrimmage. I sprinted straight downfield toward the goal line, my eyes locked straight ahead. I passed by the defender, who was defending me primarily, but also the rest of the team secondarily, and whose most advantageous position to defend against a touchdown reception once I got close to the end zone was to be between me and the quarterback. He knew I had to reach the endzone, and being behind me when I got there would do him no good at all. I was behind him now, but I wouldn't know how much distance there was between the two of us until I turned around. Not yet. I crossed the ten yard-line, then the five. I knew the ball was already in the air and closing in.

Then I crossed the goal line. *Curl in just enough to look back over your right shoulder. The ball will be right there.* I curled in just slightly toward the center of the field and looked back over my right shoulder. The ball was *not* there.

We had made two crucial errors, either of which on their own might have been surmountable, but combined, were certainly very daunting. I had not created a comfortable distance between myself and my defender. There was a small gap, probably two steps, which was enough to create a pocket into which the ball could drop safely into my hands while avoiding his. It meant that the location of the pass could be off just slightly—I had a little room to adjust—but the timing still had to be perfect. The location was perfect. The timing was not. When I turned around, the ball was still coming down, right to the spot where I was. The location was perfect, but the ball had yet to arrive, and I was still running at full stride. I had to curl completely back to the ball while waiting for it to drop from the sky, and in doing so, I skidded to my knees in an attempt to decelerate and adjust. The defender closed the gap. Time slowed down; it was one of those moments in life that are simultaneously torturous and exhilarating, and whose memories remain as intense for a lifetime. Though the ball was lancing downward toward my back-stretched hands, it appeared languid through my altered time lens.

And then it was there. Right where it was supposed to be, just a fragment of a second late. And I was right there, too, right where I was supposed to be, but stationary, not running away from the defense. But we were both there, the ball and I, just inside the goal line, at the planned point of rendezvous. We had done it. I reached out to clutch the ball and the right to play in the semifinals—the final four. We were the most improbable of teams to reach this point, a gangly band of slipshod athletes who could solve differential equations among more than thirty other teams comprised of guys who'd actually donned pads and helmets in high school while we had looked on. Hoosiers playing football. We had done it. We had won.

And just before I cradled that ball and our impossible victory in my two hands, a third hand came into view, from right to left as I faced back toward the rest of the players and the field. It reached the ball when the ball was no more than an inch or two from my fingertips, hit it hard, and deflected it to the ground. I felt ashen. That was it.

Whenever I see a perfectly executed timing pattern on television, I swell with pride, and, too, with despair. I remember that my friends and I came within inches of the same thing, even if our stage was less grand. The angst and exhilaration of that moment have faded only slightly with time. These days, twenty years later, I commute to work each day using one of three alternative routes, and when I get to Boston I pass through the city either on the Turnpike, the scenic lanes of Storrow Drive along the Charles River, or on a train. All three of those routes converge just before they reach the north endzone of our football field, and each leads me directly past it, facing the arced dormitories at the far end. I am reminded each day that these ordinary games are anybody's to play and anybody's to win.

6

SWING . . . AND A DRIVE!

Somebody once asked me if I ever went up to the plate trying to
hit a home run. I said, "Sure, every time."

—Mickey Mantle

FIRST INNING

I am on a Boeing 757 flying back to Boston from San Francisco,
where I have been on business for the past few days. My trip
coincided with the 2007 Major League All-Star Game, which was
played last night in San Francisco's AT&T Park. I did not attend
the game, although I did try to get tickets. Six hundred dollars
should buy a lot more than three hours in a ballpark. Sharing my
flight are a great many members of the Boston press corps and staff
of the Red Sox, who presumably were in attendance at the game to
watch six Red Sox peddle their wares. The guy sitting across the
aisle brandishes a 2004 World Series Ring as he reviews and anno-
tates digital video images of the game. Up in first class sits Peter
Gammons, the exalted baseball analyst for ESPN. Two rows be-

hind me near the back of the plane sits Dan Shaughnessy, the lively and controversial sports columnist for the *Boston Globe*, who recently published a book about his love of baseball, spoken in the words of a father sharing the game with his teenage son. I was so pleasantly surprised by the aura of the book because he backed out of his usual combative stance and let himself hit to all fields, skillfully reliving a thread in his life that has yet to be broken, and is both polished and tarnished with formative memories. Today he is haranguing about the heraldry, miscues, and personalities of the All-Star experience, tempered with unfettered praise for the venue, as I learn with a quick (well, drawn out) peek at his laptop while I meander purposefully back up the aisle from the lavatory. More his style and what he enjoys about being who he is.

Last night, Peter Gammons spoke on national television after the game and offered an eloquent contemplation, almost a prayer, on what has become a shameful episode in major league history. With Barry Bonds just weeks away from breaking Hank Aaron's all-time record for major league home runs, yet embattled by legal and ethical roilings stemming from his alleged steroid use, Gammons spoke with his usual communal temperance. He implored baseball fans to watch this piece of history, tarnished though it may be, and to let it revive some of the joy that is baseball, even if only by stirring up echoes of its past. Nicely put.

Watching Bonds hit his 756th home run will evoke a cascade of passions, to be sure. Many of the leviathan blasts he earned. Some of them maybe he didn't. His record-setting home run will be cathartic, and that is sometimes even more alluring than joy. Any single home run is a magnificent event, but I am not counting on Barry Bonds to bring back the joy. Mine returned in 2004. The Red Sox won the World Series that year, of course, after trailing the

New York Yankees in the American League Championship Series
by three games. Dave Roberts's stolen base, David Ortiz's multiple
walk-off hits, Johnny Damon's Game Seven grand slam, and Keith
Foulke's clinching toss to first base to win it all will resonate in
Boston for decades to come, probably generations. That brought
back the joy that is baseball, for me and for many others. And
around that same time, give or take a couple of years, in a parallel
universe of the game, I did something myself that changed my
outlook on the game.

SECOND INNING

I loved baseball when I was a kid growing up in western Michigan.
I never played little league because it never really occurred to me
that I could, but I followed my beloved Chicago Cubs all the way
down the cellar stairs each summer. I invented baseball games that
I would play for hours by myself in our backyard, throwing plastic
or rubber balls against the uneven concrete foundation wall of our
house and trying to field the random ricochets. I played on a variety
of youth softball teams with my friends and have fond memories of
playing left field in an outfield that was nothing more than dust and
gravel and of running down the first base line to beat out singles
while Mom and Dad looked on. I was a good contact hitter with a
respectable on-base percentage, even before that term came into
vogue. I was the only kid on the team who never struck out, not
even once. I was also the only kid on the team never to hit a home
run. Not even once.

I watched my father play recreation league softball during these
same years, and many more, and observed in him the same propen-

sities. He always put the ball in play—never struck out once that I can remember, and he never hit a home run. We had our share of balls hit through the outfield gaps, and we stretched out our share of doubles and triples, but we were never allowed to pass third and go home on our own merits. He once came within a foot of clearing the fence. We were both natural hitters, with only warning-track power. Of course our speed didn't help much. Most of my games as a kid were played on dirt and gravel lots with no outfield fences. Home runs were hit through the gap hard enough to just keep rolling while the batter sprinted around the base path. I was one of those kids who could pass all of the Presidential Physical Fitness tests (the pull-ups, the sit-ups, the whatnot) but never the fifty-yard dash. Not even close. What were doubles for me could have been home runs for the speedsters on the team. I comforted myself back then by thinking that I could *hit* home runs, I just couldn't *manifest* them. Most scouts see this as a significant problem. My father was the same way. When he played high school football, his team's private mantra was, "We ain't big, but we sure are slow."

There are clearly some genetic factors at work here. My father taught me the fundamentals of hitting a baseball with a wooden Louisville Slugger and an authentic hardball when I was five years old. As I write, I am teaching my own son how to hit a baseball using an aluminum Louisville slugger and a ball that's a little safer for dad. My son is about to turn five and can hit overhand pitches with some regularity. He trots around the bases regardless of where the ball lands, sometimes in the wrong direction. It only recently occurred to him that he could stop at a base and avoid being tagged, but he still gallops happily around the backyard base path collecting an outrageously inflated slugging percentage. Like his dad and his grandfather, he's a good contact hitter. Boy, will he be disappointed when he sees how far they really go. We hope that he inherits his mother's foot speed.

Baseball is only a moderate interest to my son. Ben is sometimes eager to hit a few pitches but tires of it before long and vaults himself into another random activity. You may recall that I took him to a game at Fenway Park when he was two years old. We sat in the left field grandstand and watched Curt Schilling pitch. It was 2004, the year that Schilling would pitch Game Six of the American League Championship Series against the New York Yankees with his sock bloodied from recent surgery, and, of course, the year that the Red Sox Won the World Series for the first time in eighty-six years. This was the game at which Ben turned to me after the third inning and said, "Daddy, let's go home and find Mommy."

I didn't know that history was in the making that year, but I wanted to be able to tell Ben in later years that his first game at Fenway Park went the regulation distance—four and a half innings if the home team is leading. So we agreed to watch one more inning (I can only guess at what that word meant to him at the time— maybe something opposite of outing, or outs . . . hmmmm). After four innings we bade adieu to the Green Monster and walked up the old concrete stairs toward the exits. The game wasn't official yet, so I walked slowly, and dawdled a bit when we reached the concourse that would direct us out of the park. There was only one out. I picked up Ben and held him as we watched the next two outs, which mercifully registered very quickly. I can now tell him that his first major league baseball game was at Fenway Park in the year the Sox won the World Series, and that we stayed long enough to be official.

Since that day, his interest in the game progressed for a few years. We would pass several ball fields as we drove around our town, and if a game was on, we'd often stop to watch a few innings, sometimes the rest of the game. Ben measured the game in home runs and outs—there was nothing else yet, and those were the only two potential outcomes whenever a new batter stepped to the plate. Life to a young boy is perceived in its extremes, evidently. Each evening, I would give him the Red Sox score, win or lose. We would talk about how it's all right if they don't win—the thing about baseball is that you usually get another chance. Another strike. Another at bat. Another inning. Another game. Another season. He understood, but he tempered the message just a bit. After digesting the outcome of the Red Sox game, he would ask with visible trepidation, "What did the Yankees do today?" I was not born in Boston. Ben was.[1]

THIRD INNING

A major league team, more so than other teams in other sports, carries the soul of its city through its season. Baseball provides much of the pulse of any city through the summer and early fall, and its trademark is truly bigger than life. Everybody knows what a home run is.

---

1.   Ben is almost twelve years old as I finish writing this chapter, and last year he led his Little League team in extra base hits. But he has traded in his baseball cleats for soccer cleats now, for it is on those fields where he finds most of his friends. I pressed gently for a while, but eventually realized how happy he was working with his feet. We have some good baseball memories together, and that is enough.

Many years ago, I watched a game between the Minnesota Twins and the New York Yankees in the Metrodome in Minneapolis. Sitting with me was a colleague—we were both playing hooky from a conference (where the pitching matchup was not nearly as enticing as it was at the ballpark). He was on the brink of completing a doctoral program and was a remarkably intelligent fellow. Having been born and raised in India, he was not familiar with the rules or the strategies or the pacing of a baseball game. Instead, he knew cricket. I resolved to explain the game of baseball to him as it unfolded in front of us, recognizing that it is impractical, if not impossible, to articulate the complete doctrine of baseball to an uninitiated fan without earthly examples. Terms that we take for granted are exceedingly difficult to explain to someone who did not grow up with baseball as part of the neighborhood vernacular. Try explaining the difference between purple and green to somebody who has been blind from birth. What is an out? A ball? How many outs does each player get? How long must they sit out? Where can a foul ball land so that it is not a strike? Abbot and Costello might have shed a tear. Our conversation went something like this, as best as I can recall, starting with my friend. . . .

"What a beautiful pitch!"

"Huh?"

"The pitch—really nice."

"The game hasn't started. They haven't thrown the first pitch yet."

"You mean there is more than one pitch? How far away are the other ones?"

"What?"

"The other pitches. Where are they?"

"I, uh, well . . . what do you mean?"

"A pitch—you know, the grass. It must be expensive to maintain so many."

"Ahh. Pitch. Right. No, you see, here it is called a field. A pitch is the throw to the batter."

"A throw to the batter? Oh. In cricket and soccer the field is called a pitch."

"Right, but not here. Here it is a field. We are in the Western Hemisphere. So, this is the first inning, and they are about to throw the first pitch."

"Inning?"

"Uh, right, let's see, it's like a quarter . . . no, that's not a good way to put it. Umm, a period, a bracket, a timeframe. There are nine of them in a game. Does this make sense? What do they call them in cricket? An inning is when both teams get three outs, first one team, then the other."

"What is an out?"

"Right. Anytime you do not make it safely to a base, you are out."

"So, like an injury or a cramp?"

"Well, no, not exactly. If the team in the field catches the ball before it lands, or if the ball makes it to first base before the runner, those are examples of different ways a batter can be out. The object is to hit safely."

"Without hurting anybody. . . ."

"Uh, well, yes, that's partly it. . . ."

"In cricket, a batsman is said to have lost his wicket if he is dismissed by the bowler—is that what you mean?"

"Uh, yyyeeeessss, yes, that's pretty much it. Right. But I wouldn't want to be the guy telling Vladimir Guerrero that he just lost his wicket. Heh heh."

"Who?"

"Nevermind. What, um, what exactly is a wicket, anyway?"

"Three stumps and two bails. There are two sets."

"Mmmmm. Yes. Now I remember."

(*Silence for awhile as we gaze out blankly upon the field in cognitive standby, then, moving on . . .*)

"What happens when a team gets three outs?"

"Then the other team comes to bat—it is the end of the half inning."

"What do you do if you are not getting outs?"

"You are *trying* to *not* get outs."

"What?"

"You are trying to hit the ball."

"So hits are points?"

"No, points are only scored when you make it all the way around the bases."

"Who chases the batsman around the bases?"

"What? The who?"

"The batsman. How does the batsman get around the bases?"

"You mean the batter."

"The one who strikes the ball."

"Well, ok, but you know that strikes are bad, right? You *hit* the ball. A strike is when you miss."

"How can you strike the ball and miss it at the same time?"

"No, no, no . . . wait. In baseball, a strike is when you swing and miss. You get three strikes."

"I thought you got three *outs*."

"You do. And three *strikes*."

"Which is worse, a strike or an out?"

"An out. Three strikes is one out, unless the third strike is a foul, except if it's a foul tip caught by the catcher . . . but if he drops it— uh, nevermind."

"Oh. . . . Why do they sometimes not swing?"

"You don't swing if the pitcher throws a ball."

". . . ? What else would he throw?"

"No, a ball is a pitch that is not a strike or a hit. It is too high, or too low, or not over the plate. A good batter will not swing at a ball."

"Then how would he ever hit it?"

"He waits for a strike."

"But you said that's a miss."

"Well, yes, but it is also a pitch that is not a ball—it's hittable."

(*With a nod more of apprehension than comprehension*) "How many balls before the batsman is out?"

"Batter."

"Right. Batter."

"The batter gets four balls, but that is not an out. He gets to go to first base."

"So if he doesn't swing at four pitches, he can go to first base, and if he does swing, he might be out."

"Well, yes, if the pitcher throws balls, but . . . I'm not sure I'm explaining this right. . . ."

(*We watch until a batsman is called out. I explain why, acknowledging to myself that the only way to explain baseball is play-by-play, and to make somebody spend ten years growing up with the game at every neighborhood playground.*)

"Out for the whole game? In cricket, games go on for days. That's a long time to be out."

"No, in baseball a player is only out until he is up again."

"Up?"

"Right."

". . . ?"

"Oh . . . sorry. *Up* means it is his turn to bat, like '*batter up.*'"

"When does his turn come?"

"After everyone else on his team bats."

"What if they make three outs first? Does he stay out?"

"Hey, would you like a beer or a hotdog or something?"

"No, thanks. I'm wondering why the bowler doesn't charge from the pitch before hurling at the wicket."

"What the. . . ?"

"The bowler. He just stands there."

". . . ?"

". . ."

"You mean the pitcher?"

"I guess so. In cricket, the player who hurls the ball races at the batsman from way out in the pitch."

"You mean the field. Remember, the pitch is the throw, not the grass, and bowling is something else entirely . . . where a strike is actually the best way to score points. Anyway, hmmm. That would create a lot of problems over here. If the pitcher charged the batter, he would be thrown out of the game (for the whole game), fined thousands of dollars, and you'd have to go to the bullpen a lot more often."

"I see. Is that what you call the bathroom?"

"No, no, no . . . the bullpen is where the pitchers warm up and practice when they are not in the game."

"You mean when they are out?"

"Uh, no, not exactly. Um, hmmmm. . . ."

And so it went. When such doctrinal terms as *pitch*, *ball*, and *strike* have completely unrelated and even contradictory definitions between two games, the games will forever be irreconcilable in the minds of anybody who attempts to comprehend both. Explaining baseball to a cricket enthusiast was like trying to sing Italian opera without using vowels. And I just cannot bring myself to say "wicket" at full volume. Mercifully, Bernie Williams hit a home run to left-center field in that game, and *that* I could explain. It was an epiphany for my friend, an act of near universal comprehension. A home run is not shrouded in quizzical phraseology or words with double and triple meanings. Even my son, who often ran from third to first and who for a time could not differentiate a ball from a strike until well after he swung, knew that a home run means four bases and a score. As Williams circled the bases, I said, "That, my friend, is a point." It felt heretical to diminish such an exalted achievement to a mere *point*, but in the end, I suppose that is what it amounts to.

FOURTH INNING

No, that's not true. A home run is much more than a point. It is as emblematic of the pinnacle of achievement as any single act in all of sports, and is used metaphorically throughout the English language to celebrate everything from business deals to sexual proficiency to large and inexpensive breakfast combos to sports that have nothing at all to do with baseball. Professional golfers and tennis players, male and female, derive the nicknames for their four great international tournaments from the mother of all home runs, the grand slam. Could you imagine a promotion for Tiger Woods as he is poised to capture his third of four wickets for the year? Or talking with your friend about last night's date: "Yeah, I got to the second stump but she cut me off at the bail." Don't even try to interpret that.

No, a home run is enough to turn any one of us into a baseball zealot. We have only to consider the reverberating high-pitched oration that a deep fly ball inspires day after day, season after season:

It might be. . . . It could be. . . . It is!

—Harry Caray
WGN, Chicago

Going . . . going . . . gone!

—Harry Hartman
WFBE Radio, Cincinnati

He hits it high. . . . He hits it deep . . . outta here!

—Duane Kuiper
KNBR Radio, San Francisco

In the air to deep left field . . . and that ball is gone!

—Don Orsillo
NESN, Boston

Long drive, way back, warning track, wall . . . you can touch 'em all!

—Greg Schulte
KTAR Radio, Phoenix

Swung on and there it goes! That ball is high! It is far! It is. . . .
GONE!

—John Sterling
YES Network, New York

Swing . . . and a drive. . . !

—Generic instinctive utterance
Lots of commentators, lots of cities

Forget it.

—Vin Scully
Voice of the Dodgers

Holy cow!

—Phil Rizzuto
Yankee Legend

A home run is monumental in any of its realizations. Just one,
hit at the right moment, can secure the favor and fervor of entire
cities and states for decades, and render one's foes apoplectic for
generations at the mere mention of one's name. Bucky Dent and
Aaron Boone come to mind as I write from my home in the Boston
suburbs, but so does Carlton Fisk. No other single act in sports
creates such lingering fervor, and no other can manifest itself in so
many grand gradations. Solos, two or three-run home runs, grand
slams, walkoff home runs, walkoff home runs to win a playoff
game or series, and walkoff home runs to win the World Series
transcend the hitters beyond mortality and elevate them to the stat-
ure of Hercules, Atlas, Zeus . . . or Lucifer. Very few major league
players attain these last two associations. To my knowledge, only
six men have hit walkoff home runs to win a divisional or league
championship series, and just two others have done it to win the
World Series. Bill Mazeroski of the Pittsburgh Pirates was the first

to do it in 1960, and the only man ever to hit a walkoff home run in Game Seven of the World Series. Chris Chambliss won the pennant for the Yankees when he cleared the fence in 1976, sixteen years later. Another seventeen years would pass before Joe Carter won the World Series for the Toronto Blue Jays with one swing in 1993. In 1999, Todd Pratt, substituting for Mike Piazza, sent the Mets to the National League Championship Series with a walkoff home run. And amazingly, the four years from 2003 to 2006 have each witnessed a series-winning walkoff home run. Aaron Boone (fans in Boston usually insert a colorful adjective between his first and last name in the Bucky Dent tradition) sent the Yankees to the World Series in 2003 with an eleventh-inning home run to deep left field. I turned off the television before the ball even landed, but the deed was avenged the following year when David Ortiz won the divisional series against the Angels with a tenth-inning walkoff home run, setting up the colossal comeback against the Yankees, and ultimately, Boston's first World Series title in eighty-six years. In 2005, Chris Burke of the Houston Astros ended the longest game in postseason history and won the divisional series with his eighteenth inning home run. And in 2006, Magglio Ordonez sent the Detroit Tigers to the World Series with his triumphant blast, which he delivered with two outs in the bottom of the ninth. Who's on deck this year?[2]

There have been many other sensational and timeless, even inspirational home runs, of course. Gibson, Thompson, Dent, Fisk,

---

2. Turns out it was Bobby Kielty, who started the 2007 season with the Oakland A's, and finished it in grand style with the Boston Red Sox. It was not a walk-off, but it was close. He hit a solo home run in the eighth inning of Game Four of the World Series, and that one run turned out to be the difference in a 4–3 game that clinched the Series for Boston. It was Kielty's first career at bat in the World Series. Not bad.

Jackson, Puckett, Mantle. . . . Then there are those that are logged in the everyday annals of baseball, but which are far from ordinary. When I was six years old in the mid-1970s, my father took me to see my first major league ballgame. Yankee Stadium. A Mecca for lifelong fans of the game, regardless of allegiances, but to a six-year-old who had just learned to hit with a wooden bat down at the local schoolyard diamond, it was a palace of kings with an emerald sea in the middle. On that day, one year (I believe) before he brought a pennant to the Yankees with one swing, Chris Chambliss welcomed me into major league baseball by hitting a grand slam. I knew what a home run was, but not a grand slam, and so my father carefully explained that when a home run is hit with the bases loaded, all four runners score. As an individual performance on one pitch, it cannot be bettered . . . it is one of the exalted triad that comprises the zenith of the game by virtue of an attribute that cannot be improved upon: the no-hitter, the perfect game, and the grand slam. With only slight variance in definitions, each is perfection. But from the batter's box, a grand slam is as good as it gets, and I got to witness one in person at my very first game. The Yankees lost that game 7–4 to the Baltimore Orioles, and the Chambliss grand slam accounted for the only New York scoring that afternoon, but almost forty years later I can still remember where it landed. I was hooked for life.

Over the years I have seen many more home runs, albeit less formative, from my seats in the grandstands, mostly at Wrigley Field and Fenway Park (not a bad triad itself when combined with Yankee Stadium as the prevailing venues throughout my major league viewing life). I watched Dusty Baker, when he played for the Dodgers, hit the farthest and straightest line drive home run I've ever seen, over the left field seats at Wrigley Field and across that heavenly side street named Waveland Avenue, paved with gold in the eyes of a young Cubs fan. I watched the Philadelphia Phillies give up a towering home run on the very first pitch at my very first game at Philadelphia's old Veteran's Stadium. Bernie Williams's cricket-buster has become an all-time favorite. I watched the Red Sox come back to beat the Yankees in the eighth inning with a home run over the Green Monster. Every time I have seen a home run hit before my eyes, out of the park, I marvel at how dimensionally enormous the accomplishment is. To hit a ball four hundred or more feet is the result of finely tuned body mechanics, timing, visual clarity, and raw strength. A perfect home run swing leads with the hips coming forward and pivoting sharply, but not too early. The batter then throws his hands out in front of the bat as his torso is pulled around by the hips to follow their rotation. When his hands are leading the bat, he can pull with his leading arm and push with his trailing arm, bringing their full force to bear on the ball. Then follows the bat, and then contact. Power hitters rely not just upon their arm strength, but upon this whole finely tuned and well-oiled sequence of motion that uncoils maximum body force onto the ball at the precise moment that it contacts the bat. A perfect swing is beautiful to watch, and what follows can be very liberating. A home run is a reminder that seemingly potent and fortified boundaries are often just artificial constructs, like the left-center-field wall.

Over the years, I also watched most of my teammates on various teams hit home runs, some over fences, and some that just kept rolling through the outfield gaps. I played on organized teams as a kid, in college, in graduate school—well past my prime. I was always able to hit singles with commendable regularity. I hit doubles and triples when my fly balls hit the outfield gaps, or were dropped. I can hit them to any field. But never, ever, a home run. Not one. Over time, I have developed an unspoken kinship with John Fogerty, who wrote the following lyrics to "Centerfield," his great baseball anthem:

> A-roundin' third, and headed for home,
> It's a brown-eyed handsome man. . . .

You see, I, too, have brown eyes, though that's as far as the comparison goes. As Nathaniel Hawthorne branded Hester Prynne as an adulteress with her scarlet letter *A*, so too was I marked as a respectable hitter, but with no power . . . warning track at best. And everybody knew it, which was all right, but the scarlet goose egg they made me wear on my jersey was a little ridiculous.

FIFTH INNING

Then I turned thirty-four and was invited to join a competitive slow-pitch softball league by a friend with whom I had played in graduate school. He apparently had seen my rookie card because I had never done anything spectacular on our graduate school intramural squad. He managed this recreational team, and the roster was short a player that year, and so I filled the spot. I had another chance.

Softball leagues have evolved over my lifetime. Time was when all a batter had to choose from when stepping to the plate was ash or maple. Aluminum bats have been popular for as long as I can remember. Now, though, raw aluminum is old school. The good bats today are woven, not carved or molded, from carbon fiber composites, sometimes wrapped around aluminum, sometimes not.

The materials are probably put to better use on jet engines and satellite arms, but they do indeed add some gratuitous velocity and distance to a softball. Most leagues, ours included, draw the technological line where the handle of the bat widens into the barrel. Here, quite often, the carbon cylinder is fused to an underlying aluminum core. Our regulations require that the entire cylinder be fused along the entire length, not just at its ends. A bat with an air gap between metal and carbon will provide a little too much pop, since the outer composite cylinder can deflect just slightly before transferring its elastic rebound to the ball. There is a nationally recognized organization (who actually *recognizes* them I'm not quite sure) that certifies bats for softball leagues of all levels. If the bats we use are not stamped with the seal of the American Softball Association, we could, conceivably, suffer the same fate as George Brett when he was politely asked to leave the building after hitting a home run with his bat overladen with pine tar. Whether or not anybody ever checks is not really a matter of much consequence. Suffice it to say that our ill-begotten perception of the importance of our games was enhanced by knowing that we step to the plate each inning with nationally sanctioned bats. I wonder what they allow in cricket these days. Can you strike the ball with a solar panel? Are the wickets fabricated out of titanium or do they still use hay?

Predictably during that first comeback season, I hit pretty well, but not very far. Lots of singles and some doubles, and a batting average that translated into two hits every three at bats. Our lineup was dotted with a few guys who would routinely crank the ball so far over the outfielders' heads that they could trot the bases even though the ball was technically still in play (most of the fields had no outfield fences). Whenever I managed to hit one over the outfield, it was usually a sliding double. I was jealous, no question.

And I was also resigned to the fact that if I hadn't hit a home run by my mid-thirties, well then, the rest of this sentence completes itself rather effortlessly. It is also a fairly obvious setup for the next few paragraphs.

One night late in the season, on a calm evening, I stepped to the plate in the middle of an inning, with nobody on base, and quickly collected two strikes by watching the ball sail by. I had dug in with my usual closed stance, hoping to redirect an outside pitch toward right-center field where there appeared to be a wider than usual gap.

The umpires in our league (well, one or two of them anyway) were notorious for wanting to get the games over with quickly, so that they could get home to do whatever they do after officiating ballgames. They have been known to call strikes when balls land a foot in front of the plate—a really hard call to miss. They call games off entirely if there is one too many passing cloud. Once they canceled a game at one field and not another due to rain. The fields abutted each other. They do a little jig if the players haven't all arrived within the fifteen-minute grace period at the start of each game, because the game is therefore forfeited. They call you out if you step outside the batter's box, which is delineated only in their imagination—no actual lines are painted in the dust. If you talk back, you are kicked out. Many years after the event from which I am digressing, on one of a few nights that my wife and two children made the long trip into the city to watch the game, I lifted a deep fly ball over the right fielder's head—a triple for sure, maybe more (in front of my kids!) Then, before I took my first triumphant step around the base path, the ensuing dialogue:

"Batter is out!"

". . . ?"

"Stepped out of the box."

(looking down at footprints) ". . . ?!"

"Gotta stay in the box, batter."

". . . !!"

"Next batter!"

(looking blankly at family in the stands) ". . ."

"Daddy, what happened? What did you do?"

"#**!@#$!*♂"

Aah, teaching the game to a new generation. It is no wonder that in this league, you swing at an 0–2 pitch if it is anywhere within the city limits.

I opened my stance a little, giving myself more flexibility with the oncoming pitch, wherever it might be. I am a patient batsman, and I know how to wait for the pitch I want (for crying out loud, I waited more than thirty-four years for this next one), but at 0–2, I knew I would swing at whatever came at me. By now the outcome is plainly evident, but kindly indulge me as I relive it.

Knowing that I would swing unless the ball was actually rolling along the ground took away one of the most elemental and cerebral aspects of hitting. It removed a decision, and in so doing, refined the mechanics of the swing ever so slightly by eliminating hesitancy and subsequent catch-up, or over-eagerness when you first recognize an oncoming pitch as a good one and key in on it. The coming pitch was my pitch, wherever it might fly or fall. It is mildly ironic that an 0–2 pitch in our league relieves tension and stress in the batter's box. It is the ultimate hitter's count. I relaxed and waited.

Swing . . . and a drive through the right center field gap. As I rounded first base I could see that it was still rolling and had made it past the two outfielders who were giving chase; an easy double that I could probably leg out into a triple. As I rounded second I glanced over my right shoulder to see if the throw was coming in. Not yet. Good news—I could probably go into third standing up and avoid scraping up my leg by sliding. I was wearing shorts, as were most of the players, and we all proudly brandished scabs, scars, and bloodstains from the season on our trailing shins. We played half our games, this one included, on a field built atop a converted landfill. It was a beautiful facility, an emblem of urban renewal, but we have always been more reluctant to slide into a base at this field than at the others. Who really knows what biohazards or jagged rusty scrap metal fragments might be lurking just below the dust on these base paths? Anyway, it was a worry for another day, because I was cruising around second base and starting to pull up into third . . . when the third base coach decided to send me. His eyes were wide and intense—he had been carefully watching the play develop and he knew it would be close. But as a base runner himself, he always dares the defense to make the play. With my lack of speed, he was more conservative, but at the last second, he decided I had a shot. He said it twice, very staccato, and almost under his breath when I was no more than two steps from third base, "Go. Go."

I was startled. Thirty-four years of playing ball on and off had never once led to this situation—not even an attempt. I had never passed third base of my own accord, but this time I was going to, for better or worse. I glanced at the coach, who has since become a good friend, to make sure he wasn't pulling my leg, but I knew he was serious by the way his eyes were following the ball. I also read in his face the implied message: "go hard." It was going to be close. So I dug in. I didn't have very much oxygen left, but I put the pedal down as I thumped the bag and made the final turn, me and my brown eyes.

Just me and the ball now, nothing else except trying to breathe. First one home wins. This might be the only chance I ever have, ever, to hit an official home run. Don't muck this up. As soon as I had completed the turn, I instinctively looked out over my left shoulder to see where the ball was. The second baseman had caught the relay and was in the motion of hurling the ball toward home plate. But I was halfway there now, and I could see that the throw was lagging. I hurled myself across the plate just before my legs were ready to crumble. Now I was suddenly faced with another problem. I could not stop because my knees were buckling from the "sprint" around the horn. So I ran through the plate and crashed into the backstop, which provided instant and gratifying deceleration. Safe! I was, finally, no longer the kid who had never hit a home run. It had taken thirty-four years. "Holy cow."

SIXTH INNING

There are very few stimuli that stir my soul to levels of self-awareness that diffuse or even eradicate all other sensual input. A thick fog in the predawn hours arouses an oddly intense pleasure of isolation. Add to that a cup of hot coffee softened with cream and tinged with the fragrance of wood-smoked beans, and all earthly perils are forgotten, much as they are whenever I walk through a forest after a cool rain. The smell of wood smoke from winter stoves or summer campfires turns any ill will away, as does each gradual change in season. When a woman speaks my name when addressing me, she has my attention and no words can describe the sound of that one syllable. The genuine belly laughs of my children will calm any seas that might rise in my life. These are quite simple things really, but they are the aspects of my life which, more than any others, would diminish my vitality if they were taken away. It is the same with baseball. Each game is a collection of finely tuned performances, punctuated by individual duals that are paced steadily and deliberately, allowing time for the anticipation, experience, and reaction to each one in turn as it becomes part of a greater lore. When the impossible is not happening, it is forever at the threshold. How can I not be wholly absorbed by this?

And so this singular trip around the bases became a monumental moment in my life. My career, relationships, and general outlook on life were recharged after months of numbing mediocrity, which had nothing to do with baseball. There was nobody on base when I hit the home run, so on the scorecard it was registered as one point. It was far more than that. It was like losing my virginity, but with more jubilance from the dugout and fewer apologies afterward.

SEVENTH INNING

I interrupt this fond reminiscence to report that Barry Bonds hit his 755th home run tonight, the one that tied Hank Aaron's once time-less record. He hit it about twenty minutes ago to left-center field in San Diego's brand new Petco Park. I was at Petco Park earlier this same year to watch two interleague games between the Red Sox and the Padres. The fans there are very polite, very friendly, and very tolerant, as evidenced by their graceful handling of the multitudes of in-your-face Boston fans who descended on their city. They did not quite know what to do with this home run, though.

Neither did the television commentators, who freely admitted their novice standing in such a situation. As I type this in the middle of the fourth inning of that game, still within a half hour of the big home run, the network is airing a commercial that warns young people against the destructive power of anabolic steroids. The timing is peculiar and unsettling. The tone of the evening is cathartic, to be sure. I feel a dose of relief, but nothing more positive than that. Oddly enough, Alex Rodriguez hit his five hundredth career home run earlier today, a remarkable coincidence, since he is really the only legitimate challenger of Bonds' soon-to-be new record. Because my allegiances are north of Connecticut, A-Rod's blast probably contributed to the dormancy in any joy I might have felt. But looking ahead, I'm not sure that number 756 is going to wake up the joy as Peter Gammons had hoped.

Three days have passed now since Bonds hit his record-tying home run, and tonight I went to bed late after returning home from a late summer playoff game, which we won. I had a good night statistically, but one that was wholly ungratifying. I went one for three, the one being a two-run triple in the early innings. I drove in another run on a sacrifice fly later in the game, and the box score would show that I batted in three runs and scored two myself. But I only put the ball safely in play once out of my four at bats. The first hit went straight to the second baseman. The second was the triple, a line drive through the left center field gap and into a drainage ditch. The third went straight to the pitcher (fielder's choice). The fourth went straight up and a little bit out. We won and will advance to the semifinals next week, but my lackluster performance was pestering me and has tempered some of the thrill of winning a playoff game. Two ways to look at the same thing, I suppose: three RBIs and two runs scored in a sixteen run game—not too shabby.

On the other hand, I managed just one hit in four slow-pitch at bats—pretty shabby.

It is not without other influences that I feel such internal misdirection as I am writing on this particular night. After I returned home, I watched a few innings of the Red Sox as they were getting beaten by the Angels, then went to bed, restless. I couldn't sleep, as is often the case after a game, or after a day, for that matter. My legs have fooled themselves into believing that they are actually large codfish trying to survive on land. So instead of flipping and flopping on the mattress, I got up and flipped the channels. I landed on ESPN2, which was covering the San Francisco Giants playing the Washington Nationals, and I could tell immediately that it had happened. Barry Bonds had hit his 756th home run to beat the record, about fifteen minutes before I turned on the game. He did it at his home ballpark in San Francisco, and there was a great deal of local joy. AT&T Park was the epicenter of this seismic ballgame, and tomorrow will tell how far afield the tremors were felt. As I consider the event, I realize that my natural reaction is the same as it was about my own performance on the diamond tonight—wholly dependent on context. It is a monumental accomplishment, as the telecasters painstakingly remind us far too often. And yet the crack of the bat on number 756 was also a melancholy toll of a bell that will hopefully signal the beginning of the end of a twenty-plus year era of deceit in one of our greatest and defining pastimes. That is a lot to do with one swing of the bat, but if that is what it accomplishes, it will be far more monumental than hitting a lot of dingers. As the past few days have unfolded, I realize that in lieu of joy, I simply feel a measured dose of hope that the place of this one swing in history will be more functional than nostalgic, a reminder rather than a relic. For now, its true measure is shrouded in the San Francisco fog.

SEVENTH-INNING STRETCH

Quite a series of days, these last four have been. Bonds hit the tying home run on Saturday, August 4, 2007, the same day that Alex Rodriquez hit his five hundredth. The next day, Sunday, Tom Glavine won his three-hundredth career game as a starting pitcher. He is one of only twenty-three major leaguers to achieve such a hallowed record. Two days later, on August 7, Bonds surpassed Henry Aaron as the all-time home run leader. Now, finally, we can get back to watching baseball as baseball. There are some really good pennant races underway that we should keep an eye on. I would be willing to bet that there may be some memorable home runs ahead.

EIGHTH INNING

But before this descends back into the oft-dormant void of personal reminiscence, let me borrow one more little known fact from the major leagues. Tom Glavine, he of the very recent three hundred career wins, grew up in Billerica, Massachusetts (silent *e* and a not-so-intuitive accent on *ri*), about twenty-five miles from the town that I now call home. On the night of my undefined playoff performance, the night that Bonds broke the record, I lingered at our ball field chatting with our first baseman and our pitcher long after everyone else had gone home. Turns out that our first baseman also grew up in Billerica. I knew this, and so I asked,

"Hey, you're about forty-two or forty-three, aren't you?"

"Yep."

"Did you ever bump into Tommy Glavine in high school?"

"Played with him."

". . . ! Really?"

"Backup catcher—I used to catch his warm-ups. I was one year ahead of him. Funny thing is that there were two pitchers on the team who were better than him. What he really liked back then was hockey, and he was pretty good at it. After he became a Major League star, he played in a celebrity game with the Bruins. I don't think the Atlanta brass approved that."

"Glavine isn't really a hockey name."

"Mmm. Probably right."

"He's probably only got a year or two left, wouldn't you say? Think he might want to take a whack at a few slow pitch balls one of these days? We have a few spots opening up on the roster next year. . . ."

". . . ?"

"Don't you also play in one of the same fast-pitch leagues out in Natick or Framingham that Doug Flutie plays in?"

"Yep. . . . Hmmm. Wonder what the other teams in our co-ed slow-pitch league would think if they looked out in the field next year at us and saw Tom Glavine and Doug Flutie. . . ."

Probably best to end there. Anyway, my friend has enjoyed several reunions with Tom Glavine after his Major League career was in full swing. They even played street hockey together just before Glavine's arm was valued in the multimillion dollar range, while he was still in the minor leagues, and my friend gave him a hard check. He recounted and paraphrased the brief dialogue that ensued:

"Dude, you can't do that to me, man."

"Mmm. Sorry."

My friend has heard Tom Glavine's firsthand accounts of his successes in the Major League. He is one of the greatest pitchers in the history of the game, assured to be enshrined in Cooperstown. Three hundred wins is a Herculean accomplishment. He pitched a one-hitter to win the 1995 World Series. He was named the World Series MVP. He has won two Cy Young awards. And yet, according to my friend, what Tom Glavine enjoys recounting with his high school buddies more than anything else is his single Major League home run. He hit it out of Fulton County Stadium on August 10, 1995, against John Smiley of the Cincinnati Reds. Peculiar thing, a home run. It is *way* more than just a point.

Even tonight. We played our semifinal playoff game this evening, against the setting summer sun, and we won 12–4. We were ahead 12–2 going into the final inning, but two opposing players hit towering home runs over the left field wall to close the gap a bit. The game was out of reach when the balls were hit, but there is more than one way to go out on a good note, and that's one of them. There was no question about either of these home runs from my vantage point in right field. Our left fielder drifted back out of courtesy, but they were gone the moment they left the bat. We played six or seven games on this field this year, and these two hits were the only two to clear the fence from any team including ourselves. I have far fewer misgivings about my personal performance tonight than I had in our previous playoff game, though the statistics from last week were actually better. I came up to bat twice with the bases loaded and managed to single home a run both times.

Uncharacteristically, I slid safely into third and home (not on the same play) and kicked up enough dust to actually feel just a bit fleet of foot. I also managed to catch a deep fly ball to right field that came down through the leaves of a small tree that was somehow planted on the playing surface and is considered in play. Close . . . glove . . . now. Hey, look what I got! Our defense was superb tonight, and that is what wins playoff games in softball. We held a team of strong, deep hitters to four runs over seven innings, and earned the right to play in the championship game next week, for the third year in a row. We'll cut in again for a live update when there is some news.

As was the case last week, it is not without other influences that I feel so jubilant tonight. I drove twenty-six miles home after our game in the city and arrived in my living room just in time to see Jason Varitek slide across home plate on a walk-off single by Coco Crisp. The ninth-inning Red Sox rally was triggered by none other than a home run, a solo by Mike Lowell onto Landsdowne Street (Boston's toast to Waveland Avenue in Chicago) to tie the game. All was not well, though. I learned that Phil Rizzuto, the lifelong Yankee player and commentator, passed away today. No matter where your allegiance lies, baseball took a hit today. Holy cow, Phil. Well done.

TOP OF THE NINTH

Back now in time a few years to our softball field. When we are not playing atop that converted landfill, we have the fine fortune of playing on another newly converted field, although this one actually used to be a ball field before it was restored to a ball field . . . a nicer one. The City of Cambridge takes great pride in this complex of three diamonds—two fenced Little League parks and a larger, open softball field. The recreation department actually paints fresh foul lines on the softball field (still no batters boxes, though) and sifts the infield dirt with heavy screens dragged behind all-terrain-vehicles on the afternoons of game days. I've seen them do it. Come playoff time, they fill in the ruts with fresh dirt, real dirt, baseball dirt, dusty dirt that's also gritty. All of this makes us feel more like minor league prospects than Tuesday-night rec-league roustabouts, but the league is competitive and the city tips its hat to the game by maintaining its facilities to near professional standards. There is a modern drainage system underneath the field which siphons away standing water with impressive speed. The dugouts are covered by awnings. The grass is never too long. And there is the left field fence.

That tantalizing fence that starts two hundred and seventy feet down the left field line and slices out into left field, arcing devilishly away from home plate. It is the fence of the adjoining Little League field, and was never really intended to function as a boundary for the softball field, though it most certainly does. Part of it, anyway. It arcs away so acutely to encircle the adjacent field that it is functionally impenetrable beyond about sixty feet off the left field foul line. But from the plate of the softball field it looks like the Green Monster, straight and stoic across left field, almost within reach. On most nights, the southwest winds render our wall an impenetrable fortress, but on nights when the wind is low, or when it wisps in from the north, it is awfully hard not to try to pull the ball hard to left field.

Every year, a few balls will sail over that fence and the guys who hit them will trot the bases to the cheers of their teammates.

We won a semifinal game a few years ago on a fence-clearing three-run home run. Tom Glavine's buddy cleared it twice in one game that same year. It happens less frequently now, since the league instituted "restricted flight" balls last year. These balls counter some of the technology in the approved bats with their softer core, and simply don't travel as far as would a more tightly wound ball. Bringing a top-of-the-line bat to a game in our league is a bit like filling a Ferrari with leftover lawnmower gas. It will run, but . . .

When I hit my home run a few years earlier, it had been through an outfield gap on a field that had no fence. Well, technically it had a fence. Barry Bonds *might* be able to clear it. It never factored into the games, it was so far away. My home run may have bumped up against it after rolling and rolling, but nobody has ever cleared that fence to my knowledge. As good as it felt to have circled the bases, as transforming a moment as that was, there remained a lingering and gnawing question. What does it feel like to trot the bases? Any triple or home run I hit happens because a line drive slices through the gap and keeps rolling. I simply did not, do not, have the power to clear our left field monster, and so I gaze at it longingly from the dugout, and again whenever I step to the plate, and then usually plant my feet to aim away from it. I'm a directional contact hitter, and pretending to be anything else results in pop-ups to the short-stop or dribblers to the pitcher. How many times must I learn this lesson?

PITCHING CHANGE

We won our league championship game on that field tonight. It was our second championship in three years, and we won it going away, sixteen to five. I think everyone on the team scored at least one run. The game was actually over in the first inning when we scored eight runs, punctuated by none other than a three-run home run by our pitcher (he of the ilk that sends runners home on close plays when coaching third base, as he once did to me). He sliced the ball through the right-center field gap and slid home just as the tag was applied. I was standing just behind the plate, having scored from first base, and turning, I saw our pitcher bearing down and the ball clearing the outfield on its way home. They reached the plate at the same time, give or take, and the tie went to the runner. And they say pitchers can't hit. Tom Glavine would be proud. I listened to the fourth movement of Beethoven's Ninth (both the top and bottom) on my long drive home, recounting the whole team's highlights from the season in my mind while the majestic chorale played triumphantly. Better than drugs. I could even hear the exact spot where I popped up to the shortstop at my third plate appearance.

But nobody on either team cleared the fence tonight, even though the wind was blowing straight out. The final batter for the other team came close. Our left fielder caught the final out with only a few feet to spare, and was awarded the game ball for a fine all-around performance. It is really hard to hit the ball over that fence.

But there was one night before the era of restricted flight balls. It was a late summer night, and our team was putting the finishing touches on a dismal season. It was the season just after I had hit my solitary career home run, and just prior to the midwinter barroom

meeting at which we revamped half of the lineup and followed it
the next season with what, to us, has become fondly known as "The
Season." We had won perhaps only one or two games all year, and
we were playing a team against whom we had never even been
competitive. They were mean, arrogant, and strong, but they were
also slow. Even I could outrun them, and looping a ball anywhere
onto the outfield grass was a ticket to extra bases. But we couldn't
do it. They were magnets, and we always hit the ball right at them.
It was maddening, and perhaps that is why I chose to do something
that I had never done before. I decided to pull the ball hard that
night, down the left field line. It is not normally my strength. My
power alley is to straightaway center, and when I pull the ball to
left field, I usually fly out or settle for a single. I have an uncanny
ability to hit the ball to the exact spot on the field where the left
fielder stands, wherever that may happen to be on a given night. He
will take a step or two, open his glove, and I'll walk back to the
bench. But I knew that if I could place one down the line, I'd have
an easy double, maybe a triple, because their left fielder was the
slowest of their outfield pack. Why not? We were down by almost
ten runs and the game was nearly over. Might as well have a little
batting practice.

So I stepped to the plate and dug in with a wide-open stance,
sacrificing some torque for some directional certainty. A closed
stance would let me uncoil more powerfully, using the term quite
loosely, but that extra body mechanic takes a lot of practice and
experience that I do not have. Any scout would realize that the
position of my feet is a dead giveaway to where I'm aiming and for
the kind of pitch I am waiting for. But absent a scouting report,
fielders generally do not adjust themselves into defensive shifts in
our league based solely on foot position. So I waited somewhat

lethargically for a pitch on the inside corner, belt high, the only kind of pitch that I can turn on effectively. If I didn't get it after two strikes, I would close the stance a little bit and be ready for a broader array of pitch locations.

The first pitch came in. I didn't like it. Strike one.

The second pitch came in. Still no good. Strike two.

Hitter's count. I gave up on shooting the ball down the left field line and closed my stance a bit, still leaving it open just enough to try to pull the ball anyway, just not down the line. Their left fielder really was slow, and I was aching to capitalize on this, just once. As I said earlier, in this league, you swing at an 0–2 pitch or you turn around and drag your bat back to the dugout. So I watched and waited for the next one, bat cocked. There was a subtle breeze at my back.

A good pitcher will waste a pitch in a situation like this, knowing that the batter is likely to swing at anything, even junk. Not this guy. He sent me a melon over the inside corner, belt high, as if I had ordered it off a menu. It was almost too perfect, the kind of pitch for which I lose patience and swing at too early and skim the underside of the ball, which then flops limply to the pitcher or the shortstop. But not this time. With the ultimate hitter's count in this league, I was relaxed, and I waited. This was not a clutch hit, and no matter what happened, we were going to go home with another tick in the loss column. Relax. Wait for it. Here it comes . . . oh yeah, this is perfect . . . and . . . now.

Hitting a ball solidly, right in the sweet spot of the bat, is one of the most viscerally satisfying feelings of which I am qualified to speak, at least without risking the prospect of public burnings of my writing on New England town commons. You hardly feel the contact, and the bat never slows down, waivers, or transmits any shock to the batter's hands and wrists. The swing is through the ball, not at it. My hips and hands led the bat, and the ball started sailing toward left field, high and deep.

I watched it as I trotted down the first base line, wholly expecting the left fielder to take a few backward steps, wait for it, and catch the ball. It was heading right toward him, after all, but I could see that it would at least back him up a little. I was watching the ball instead of running hard, and I remember seeing the sidespin as it passed over the infield and arced into the outfield.

Away from the plate and about half way down the first base line, I had a little better perspective on the ballistics of my hit, and I could see that I had really gotten all of this one. With my warning track power, it just might plop in behind the left fielder's head, so I stepped up my speed a bit, not that anyone could have noticed the differential, and kept watching the ball. And then, very suddenly, as the ball was arcing downward, I realized what was happening. This one had a chance. It had a chance to go where no ball of mine has ever gone. That black chain-link monster didn't budge. It still looked like an impenetrable fortress, but the left fielder had his back to the infield and was sprinting toward the fence. And then, just as suddenly as I had realized that this ball had a chance of clearing the yard, he slowed up to a jog without turning around. That is how I knew. The ball was still in flight, but I knew. I do not recall actually seeing the ball land on the other side of the fence. I believe I looked down at the dirt the moment I knew, my natural tendency when receiving good news, as if to physically contain it with inward withdrawal for a moment. I stepped on first base, made the turn, and then looked up to see the ball rolling around on the little league field across the fence. Got it.

I slowed down again, not hard to do, and began the jog that had eluded me for a third of a century. My face must have worn the grin of a seven-year-old kid, because even the second baseman seemed to realize that this was a lifetime achievement for me, and shook my hand as I passed by. I slapped hands with the third base coach as I rounded the final corner, but to save my life, I cannot remember who it was. I thought for a minute that I saw Saint Peter as I crossed home plate, but it was just the umpire, who graciously muttered, "nice shot." It was over too quickly. I remember touching each of the bases, but nothing in between them. I wanted to run the circuit again, but turned, still running, into our dugout to receive some genuine good will from my teammates. The home run had no impact on the game or the season. We lost the game and the season was a disaster. But never again would I wonder if I had it within me to go the distance in the game that is one of the loves of my life.

DIGRESSION BY THE COLOR COMMENTATOR

Speaking of lifetime achievements, twenty-three year old Clay Buckholtz of the Boston Red Sox pitched a no-hitter tonight against the Baltimore Orioles. It was his second major-league start. He was still in the minor leagues just yesterday. His record is 2–0. He probably has a future in the big leagues. Perhaps he will be the next Tom Glavine, if he plays in enough interleague games to crank a ball over the fence someday, just once. If it doesn't work out for him, we'll hold a roster spot open on our softball team, just in case. He can bat cleanup after Flutie.

BACK TO THE GAME

Now, here is an odd thing. I am a vivid dreamer, not the fantasy type of dreams (ok, those too), but the real, nighttime, Technicolor productions that destabilize my psyche such that throughout the following day, half of my brain actually believes the events happened. This has produced some tense moments at meetings, let me assure you, and my eyes are particularly shifty as I encounter people in real life who also wend their way through my nocturnal misconstructions of the world. It is oppressive enough that my dreams are so convincing; the fact that some of them occur time after time must surely have degenerative effects on my health. At one point in my life, I had one of my recurring dreams analyzed by a psychiatrist. In the dreams, I would find myself floating in outer space clinging to an enormous bubble that very clearly, to me, represented a monumental task that had been assigned, but which I knew I would not, and could not, ever begin because it could not ever be finished. I always found myself, in these dreams, clutching desperately to this gigantic bubble immediately after learning what the assigned task would be. The tasks were never really that strenuous, but always involved doing the same thing more than once, and in their repetitive nature, they became psychologically paralyzing. In one instance my task was to count a hundred chairs in a room. In another, I had to affix three wheels to a plastic model of a helicopter. In the dreams, the assigned tasks instantly morphed into this smothering bubble, which all but devoured me as I held onto it for dear life and drifted helplessly through the galaxy. The honorable psychiatrist believed that this bubble represented something quite different, quite less abstract, and I quickly terminated our arrangements when his line of questioning started to suggest that I had more in common with Oedipus Rex than I would care to think about. He was, to borrow a baseball metaphor, off base. Hey, I was there, at least metaphysically, and I know this was not Sophoclean. Anyway, I have many other recurring dreams, most of them unpleasant, some of them not so much. Some of the recurring dreams are sports dreams in which I fail spectacularly. I will miss an open layup in a Final Four game, twice. I always get my own rebound and miss again before being engulfed by the defense as they finally reach my end of the floor. Football too. I am wide, wide open, way downfield, always on the left sideline . . . and the ball goes through my hands. My baseball dreams are no less fraught with indignity. I have dreams in which, for example, the whole outfield is playing on the infield, or is clustered in left field. All I have to do is hit away from them, but I always send the ball directly into the centroid of the lopsided cluster of humanity on the field. I recall only one or two successful sports dreams from a lifetime of nocturnal duress, but that changed on the night before I hit the home run over the fence. On that night, the night *before* it actually happened, I dreamt that I stepped to the plate on that very field, swung, and watched the ball sail right over that very fence. I dreamt that I trotted gracefully around the base path, slapped hands with the third base coach, and landed triumphantly at home plate. I had never had a dream like that before that night, and it has never repeated itself. Neither has the actual home run that followed the next evening. Go figure that one out. I bet that never happened to Oedipus Rex. I do know this: if I ever do manage to catch that elusive football or make either of those two lay-ups in dreamland, I'm calling an agent the next morning.

BOTTOM OF THE NINTH

This all seems, perhaps, a bit self-indulgent, and perhaps it is. But, after all, the premise of this collection of memoirs is to remind myself how infrequently great moments happen, and how they can happen on any stage. Nevertheless, I am compelled to dilute some of this verbal champagne with the *whole* truth. You will recall that all through grade school, I was the kid who never hit a home run, and who never struck out. It was true through college and graduate school, with one quasi, nagging, deflating exception. In an intramural softball game in college, I actually did strike out, once, but I am still challenging this statistic with every legal and regulatory means at my disposal, which is to say that I have all but forgotten about it and don't really consider it to be legitimate. You see, in that league, every batter started each at-bat with one ball and one strike, even before the first pitch was thrown. Many leagues do this in an effort to speed up the games and to provide mediocre athletes like me the necessary asterisks to affix to our statistics as we deem appropriate. To strike out on two strikes is like getting a warning from a state trooper for driving five or six miles an hour over the highway speed limit. Sure, it's a violation, but really, c'mon. So, my solitary lifetime strikeout had an asterisk next to it. . . .

Until last year, when I was thirty-seven years old. I stepped to the plate in our semifinal game. We had come back after trailing by eight runs to take a commanding lead, and at this midway point in the game, it was all but over. Everybody on the team had hit at least a triple, as we like to remember it, and that was actually not far from the truth. Now, I'm no Casey at the Bat, not even close, but a few choice verses of Earnest Lawrence Thayer's famous poem came to mind on that evening:

> And now the leather-covered sphere came hurtling through the air,
> And Casey stood a-watching it in haughty grandeur there.
> Close by the sturdy batsman the ball unheeded sped—
> "That ain't my style," said Casey. "Strike one!" the umpire said

Apparently, Thayer exhibited some leanings toward cricket. Notwithstanding my literary criticism, I clutched the bat and watched the first pitch sail by, taking all the way as I often do with the first pitch just to settle in. It was a strike, and I had no argument with the call. Then came pitch number two.

> With a smile of Christian charity great Casey's visage shone;
> He stilled the rising tumult; he bade the game go on;
> He signaled to the pitcher, and once more the dun sphere flew;
> But Casey still ignored it, and the umpire said "Strike two!"

All right, there was very little Christian charity on my face, even though we had a commanding lead, and there was no rising tumult from the stands that needed to be quelled. But the rest of the verse was spot on. The second pitch was not to my liking, so I watched it sail past and heard the umpire bark, "Strike two!" So I found myself in the enviable position of being down in the count 0–2. Ahh, sweet freedom. Not so with Casey:

> The sneer has fled from Casey's lip, the teeth are clenched in hate;
> He pounds with cruel violence his bat upon the plate.
> And now the pitcher holds the ball, and now he lets it go,
> And now the air is shattered by the force of Casey's blow.

You know the rest. With a tip of the hat to Thayer and his classic poem, let me offer a personal reprise of this particular verse as it replays in my own mind from time to time:

> Westphal's sneer was comical, his show of force benign,
> He knew that he'd be swinging without checking for the sign,
> And now the pitcher holds the ball, and now he lets it go,

And Westphal swings and misses, and to no-one, mutters, "D'oh!'"

With that swing I erased the asterisk next to my one career strikeout so completely, so resolutely, that the metaphorical paper tore right through. I missed that pitch so badly, so awkwardly, that I still wonder if some of the pain in my lower back is a remnant of the imbalance and conflicting mechanics of that swing. I did not hear anything pop, in fact I heard nothing at all but the whiff of the bat through the empty air . . . followed by an onslaught of cat calls from the dugout. Destitute and head hanging in mortal shame, I trudged back to the dugout to face my jury, all of whom had grins the size I'd worn when I'd cleared the fence that one solitary time. The batter who followed me, Glavine's old buddy, cleared the fence in left field. I watched a phantom of myself circle the bases with a relaxed gait and cross the plate, turning to congratulate the batter upon his arrival . . . all in my mind, because I had struck out and was absent on the base path. Oh well, I think I hit a couple of triples in that game to bookend my spectacular strikeout, so I shuttled through the standard psychological reactions to life-altering trauma pretty quickly: disbelief, denial, avoidance, cursing, outrage, punching trees, name-calling, and finally gratuitous acceptance. It only took an inning and a half, and a cheap beer after the game.

GAME RECAP

In the end, I will be able to look back on my life and make the following claims: It took me twenty years to find the girl I would marry. I took thirty years to decide on a career. It took thirty-three years to produce my first offspring. It took me thirty-four years and the introduction of space-age technology to hit my first home run, thirty-five years to clear the fence, and thirty-seven years to register one (and two-thirds) strikeouts. Each one was worth the wait.

7

ALL IN

"**M**y grandfather's name was Carlo and my parents named me after him. My mother said he was the most dignified man she ever knew, tall and elegant, hardworking, smart and honest. He was really good looking, too, with thick dark hair and a deep dimple in his chin. He looked a lot like the actor Cary Grant and in some circles people called him that as a nickname. Grandma says even into his eighties women would flirt with Papa (grandfather), but he never ever flirted back. Papa said that would be wrong and undignified.

"Papa was born in Italy and came to this country when he finished high school, at age eighteen. That was a really brave thing to do. Even though he wasn't yet a citizen, he proudly served in the Korean War. America was his adopted home and although Rome was his hometown and his mom still lived there until she died a few years ago, America was more important to him than anywhere in the world. Papa was a self-made man. Relatives of his taught him the construction trades. He went to Wentworth and one professor there was so impressed with his knowledge that he offered him a teaching job. Papa specialized in ornamental plastering and his company was the number-one company in eastern Massachusetts. His work is still seen in public buildings, historic buildings and even in the Boston Public Garden.

"There were a lot of reasons to admire him for how he conducted himself and for his work ethic. He taught me things and spent a lot of time with me and always made me feel like I was the most important person in the world. When I would visit, sometimes Papa would let me help him tend his rose garden. He was a master rosarian and his garden won first place from Mayor Menino's Best Gardens in Boston one year for his neighborhood.

"He said that the most important thing in his life was his family and that he would rather be in his wife and children's company than with anyone else. That was wonderful to hear because Papa and Grandma were really well-known in Boston and everyone knew them from the governors to the mayors to billionaires to John F. Kennedy when he was a senator. They were always being invited to really fancy parties, and they gave such fancy parties, too, but for Papa his family was all that mattered. He said when you took care of your health and always chose your family over anything else, then you had everything important in the world."

Quite a man and quite a life, I would say, dedicated to country, to family, and to principles. Dedicated entirely.

But wait until I introduce you to his grandson, the eleven-year-old narrator up to this point. It will be in knowing him that we shall learn more about his patriarch, his namesake. And perhaps more importantly, in hearing him speak of how and why he knew his grandfather the way he did, we will also learn who this young man is. We will learn why he, too, will someday have a grandson who compares him to a pop star, and why his branch on the family tree will be equally sturdy. The heirloom of this family is its dignity.

This boy is known as Giancarlo. You can already see the steadfast Italian endurance of his grandfather's name. I met him one drizzly Sunday morning at one of our town's youth baseball diamonds. He had just moved with his family into town and thought that playing springtime baseball would help him meet some classmates for the coming fall. He was tall for his age and disarmingly charming, with a constant smile borrowed partly from Harry Potter and partly, I imagine, from his grandfather. He told me that he worried because he had taken a few years off from baseball and was not sure he would measure up to the talent at his grade level.

Our town's founding fathers (rather, the Little League Board of Directors) had somehow conferred upon me the unholy task of ranking the athletic prowess of preschoolers to pre-teens, and placing them in appropriate divisions and leagues, and ultimately teams. I could never tell if I felt more like a commissioner or a badly uninformed and underpaid talent agent. But despite the ambiguities of my own identity, this young man was very resolute in his purpose on that Sunday morning. Having not played for a couple of years, and having missed the tryouts due to the timing of the family's move, he and his mother and I wanted to make sure he could play safely with his would-be classmates instead of under-classmates. In junior high, such underlings can be a collective anathema, but this was not Giancarlo's concern. He simply wanted to play ball to meet other boys he would see in his own school hallways and classrooms.

To set him at ease, I told him that many kids take a few years off, as they try different sports or just want breaks from outrageous over-commitments they (or their well-meaning parents) make. I told him what I expected of an eleven-year-old ball player. First, at such an age, if you are playing baseball for any reason other than to enjoy yourself with friends, you are on the wrong field. That said, there are basic skills that players should exhibit so that they can accomplish two fundamental goals of the game: live to play the next one, and do something, even once, to contribute to the enterprise. Such a mantra establishes both hope and self-confidence, and of course, gives these virtues ample time to age.

The skills I wanted to see were very basic, and had more to do with self-preservation than contributing to highlight reels. Beginning at age seven or eight, Little League players play with hardballs, and by the time they reach age eleven and twelve, some of them can throw close to seventy miles an hour. Most fathers reading this will naturally cringe, for we have all been in carnival cages that measure the mediocrity in our own fastballs. Admit it. We throw out our shoulder with a vicious heave, stifle the scream, turn the grimace into translucent bravado, and strut around proudly awaiting the result while shaking out the pain searing down through our elbow. And then it's flashed in lights: forty-seven miles-per-hour. You have all been there, and I know it because I've seen you, and I've been you. (For what it's worth, it's because we don't use our legs, or our hips, or our minds. Let's not kid ourselves—we are trying to impress the other kids in the line, and their dads, and probably their moms.) But some well-coached eleven-year-olds can throw a good fastball, and good hitters can send it hither and yon (mostly yon) even faster. Players must be able to protect themselves from such artillery with nothing more than an aluminum stick and a leather mitten. Such is the armor of our day.

We began by playing catch, first with a tennis ball, and then with a hardball once I could see that he had enough command of his glove. I gradually increased the speed of my throws, stopping just short of my blistering one-time record of fifty-one miles-per-hour (in college). Giancarlo didn't catch everything, but he knew how to position his glove, and more important, when to back away. He could also throw back to me with reasonable consistency, and so I asked him to man the shortstop position for a while. I hit him some ground balls and popups, some intentional, some by chance. Again, his glove work was solid, but his footwork needed some practice in both directions—getting to the ball, and when necessary, getting away from it. These are not uncommon traits in eleven-year-old ball players, and they would simply require a good coach, legions of which our town enjoys in abundance.

Lastly, I gave him a bat and asked him to hit my thirty-four mile-per-hour fastball, the best I can do when pitching ten or more balls in rapid succession without needing surgery. Many players are surprised when I tell them that hitting a baseball has more to do with footwork than with arm strength. (Incidentally, I give the same advice to aspiring outfielders, who are often surprised to learn that fly balls do not angle their trajectories graciously into outstretched gloves). A good coach can take a kid who doesn't know which end of the bat to hold and teach him or her to hit in an afternoon if the player learns to take a small step with the swing. Without the step, a young hitter has no balance because the swinging bat wants to pull him over, no timing because there is no decisive initiating movement, and no power because half the body remains listless. We worked a bit on reestablishing the basics of balance and stepping into the swing before tossing any balls.

Some coaches at this level, many of whom may be cringing by now, begin coaching major league hitting before its time, when the lead foot pivots instead of steps, and the power then follows from the rotation of the hips. This is called rotational hitting, as opposed to the linear hitting that I was taught forty years ago, when a batter simply steps into the pitch and relies on the momentum of shifting weight to achieve power. Of course, back then goalies didn't wear masks, either, but who am I to distinguish progress from stability? These days, good ball players almost unanimously favor rotational hitting the way basketball players favor shorts to the mid-shin. But it's harder to teach and not as intuitive or as immediately productive as taking a simple step forward into the swing. As well as I can understand it, the differences are roughly analogous to those of Newtonian and Quantum physics. In my day, I studied and professed Newton's basic laws of motion, so I still hit and teach with a straight step because it results in rhythm and balance. With young players, these virtues are much more important than power or grace or dark matter. I will never stop coaching kids to take a small step into the pitch until they are confident and consistent hitters. Then, and only then, should they try to hit like Albert Pujols, the All-Star certain Hall-of-Famer for the Cardinals and Angels who has perhaps the best rotational hitting motion in the game.

After three or four flat-footed swings, Giancarlo caught on to what I was saying and began stepping into the pitches and swinging with better balance and precision. He was remembering his earlier years of playing, and I could see that he was immediately coachable—he listened. Perhaps more than anything I saw in him that day, I saw that he listened and responded. He was entirely present in what he was doing and in what I was saying. Entirely present. While I appreciated this, as any coach would, I had no idea yet that this rare attunement was actually the heart of his young character. For now, I simply noted that he hit about 30 percent of my pitches, smiling equally at contact and at misses, not too proud, not too worried. Besides, this was a batting average worthy of any major leaguer regardless of how they shuffle their feet.

And so I shook his hand and thanked him for coming out to the field with me that day, telling him that it had been a pleasure meeting such a well-mannered young man and aspiring player. My daughter had come with me that morning to help shag flies and I asked her to play a little catch with Giancarlo while I spoke with his mother for a moment.

"He did just fine," I announced in a quiet voice by the dugout. "He isn't a superstar, but neither was I ever a superstar, and I've enjoyed playing baseball for many years. He will be all right playing with kids his age, but I'm glad you were willing to check this out. It's important for safety reasons—we need to know that kids understand how hard and fast that little ball can fly."

"That's what he wants. He likes the game, but mostly, he just wants to get to know some of the boys he'll see in the classroom this fall."

"Things begin to get a little competitive at this age, probably more than they should. Play catch with him in the backyard whenever you can so that he gets even more confident with his glove. I'm glad he decided to play again this year, and I hope that he has a great experience."

And then she told me why Giancarlo had taken two years off from the game. I remember being silent for a moment, then turning to look at the young man playing catch with my daughter out by second base, smiling and laughing together. It was then that I began to see beyond a young eleven-year-old ball player relearning the fundamentals of baseball. I began that day to understand dignity, in the picture of two young kids tossing a baseball back and forth. Papa would have understood, too.

And so I placed Giancarlo on a team with other boys his age. Because he was older than both of my children who played on teams with kids their age too, I never got to see him play while I was coaching my own offspring. And so two weeks into the season, I wrote to his mother to ask how things were going. I received a disheartening reply that made me lament that the competitiveness of youth athletics can sometimes stifle the social advantages we hope our children gain when they suit up as one of a team. I also wondered at my own naivety, and how perhaps with wishful thinking I had put Giancarlo either in harm's way, or unwillingly into an experiment in social equity.

"He's been bullied by some of the other kids on the team because he isn't playing as well as they are," his mother told me. In these enlightened days, the term "bully" has broadened to include all forms of abuse, and thankfully there had been no physical intimidation. But the better players on the team were teasing him about skills that I had deemed adequate, but which were failing to satisfy the harsher judgment of athletic peers in a new town. Giancarlo was seen as the new kid, and not one of the team.

> Papa was born in Italy and came to this country when he finished high school, at age eighteen. That was a really brave thing to do. Even though he wasn't yet a citizen he proudly served in the Korean War.

I wonder how his platoon-mates treated him.

Months later, when I had a chance to talk with Giancarlo about his experience, I asked him about these first few weeks. I was particularly interested because like him, I had been a good-natured and friendly kid, and I endured both verbal and physical bullying from a schoolmate when I was exactly his age. It took me many months to gather the courage to stand up to him, or even to persuade myself of the triviality of his scoffing. Once I did, he never troubled me again, but the experience terrified me and dragged out for so long, that even today, I bristle at the sight of a fist or an intimidating word. Without leading the question with this subject matter, I asked simply, "How were you feeling as part of this team at the beginning?"

"I took some teasing for being not up to their standards, but I think that was because the other guys were so intent on winning. On one hand, I felt bad thinking that maybe I was letting them down, but on the other hand, they didn't always get on base, either." He also told me that he had won a karate trophy when he was five years old in front of a thousand people, but I imagine he kept this to himself inside the dugout. I envied his confidence. A preteen facing tough guys is a cruel situation. I know. But to Giancarlo, his would-be adversaries were simply teammates with lackluster on-base percentages. He wanted simply to earn their trust and respect, as teammates now, but eventually as classmates, perhaps friends. The eleven-year-old in my own life story wondered how different my teenage years might have been had I borrowed his outlook earlier than I had. I never quite rose above the insipience of the schoolyard social hierarchy.

But before I talked with Giancarlo about his reactions to all this, I spoke with his coach. He told me a few things I already knew:

"I love having Giancarlo on my team. He's one of the nicest kids I've ever met, and always a good sport. He is also one of the most coachable kids I have ever known (one of my very first perceptions, you may recall). He doesn't get too many hits, but that doesn't matter because he finds ways to contribute in the field and in the dugout. I have noticed the ribbing he gets sometimes, but he lets the comments from his teammates roll off his back and just works harder than anyone. I will watch the interactions very carefully, but so far I haven't needed to intervene."

I would speak to his coach again in two weeks, about another side of baseball. For now, I felt satisfied leaving the situation in his capable hands, and replied, "He tells me that he was a really good player when he first started the game, but took time off for a while so I'm glad you can help him back into the game, and even use his attitude to coach others. Do you know, by the way, why he took those couple of years off? May I tell you?"

Giancarlo stopped playing baseball for two full years. He stopped karate lessons, swimming, and golf lessons, too. He stopped music lessons for two years, and this may have been his most difficult sacrifice. His father is an operatic baritone who has performed at the Metropolitan Opera in New York, and his mother is a classical music aficionado, with a weakness for classic rock and groups like The Police, which instantly endeared her to me. Strings and Sting in equal measure. But Giancarlo had to put his saxophone, his bat and clubs, and his belt aside. These were the trimmings of his every week, the accents and overtures of childhood, the culmination of each grand crescendo toward the weekend. He loved them all. But he loved people more. I learned Giancarlo's story in part through an e-mail he sent to me one day, explaining some of the choices in his young life. We had tried to find time to talk in person about his season, but the gears and sprockets of our individual lives could not quite find the necessary synchronicity (despite how good that album was). And so we wrote to each other.

I received his note on a dreary afternoon sitting alone in the basement of a hospital in Boston waiting to have my knee x-rayed in preparation for reconstructive surgery later that month. The waiting room was at the end of an invisible corridor that bent away and was known only by the reverberating footsteps of occasional staff tending to their imagined duties. I was the only one waiting. It was the Christmas season, and amidst the windowless cinder block drear of my surroundings and the looming holiday rehab, I was feeling rather sorry for myself. I knew by this time why Giancarlo had taken the two years off, but this was the first time I heard it in his words: "When you love someone and they have no hope left you have to be their hope." Two years ago, Papa had been diagnosed with the lung cancer caused by asbestos: mesothelioma. And so Giancarlo set his childhood aside and devoted every single weekend for two years to be at the side of his beloved grandfather. Alone in the basement of the hospital, entombed for an afternoon within the walls of my own selfish depression, tears ran down my cheeks as I read Giancarlo's words.

"When Papa got sick in March (two years ago), baseball was just beginning, but I couldn't go there and have fun knowing that he was lying in the hospital. My mom said we didn't know how much time we'd have with Papa and she left it up to me when I came, but I told her I needed to be with him more than ever. I figured that my friends would understand, that baseball and all my other activities would still be there later on, but I was only going to have my Papa for a little while. It wasn't something I had to think about and I didn't think I was doing anything 'special.' Papa came first."

Papa had always been important to Giancarlo, as evidenced by his opening narration in this piece. Even before the diagnosis, the two of them would spend frequent time together. They would tend the roses together, watch old black-and-white westerns in Papa's big recliner, or read together. Papa taught his grandson how to use tools and how to do crossword puzzles, hard ones, in ink. Then, "he started to slow down, really slow down, the year before he was diagnosed with the cancer. We didn't do too much physical stuff that year because he would get tired, but we did do a lot of snuggling in the recliner. We didn't have to say much to each other. We just knew how to be with each other even when we were quiet. I would put my head and my hand over his heart and his heartbeat told me everything I needed to know."

And when Papa was confined to the hospital with terminal cancer, it was Giancarlo's turn to speak, and his voice became his entire being, setting aside all of the usual distractions of youth. "Mom told me back then that it gave him great comfort to see me smiling at him. I couldn't make his cancer go away, but I could hold his hand and tell him about my week and try to make him laugh and give him hugs and kisses." Giancarlo would hand his grandfather glasses of water and hold cold compresses on his forehead. Other kids were outside playing while Giancarlo tended a special garden in its twilight.

"In the last month of Papa's life, he couldn't talk because of the tubes they put down his throat. I could tell he was really sad about that but I think we had already said everything we needed to say. On the weekend before he died he was in and out of consciousness. I needed to tell him one more time how great he was as a man and role model and at being my Papa. I always told him I loved him but I wanted to say it one more time. His nurse said even if he didn't respond he could definitely hear me, so I held his hand and talked right into his ear. Once I had the chance to do that, I felt really calm. I also told him "thank you" and that was important for me to do. Winning baseball games, or even if we didn't win but knowing I played my best—that felt great and every kid will tell you that. But holding Papa's hand one more time, Mr. Westphal, saying I love you and thank you for everything, beat everything."

And then Papa passed on, with these final blessings from his Grandson. Giancarlo, dignified by his complete devotion and satisfied by the riches of shared time and words, once again proudly hung a baseball jersey on his sturdy shoulders. Papa had loved baseball and had loved watching him in uniform in younger years. He had heartily encouraged young Giancarlo to always do his best, for therein lay the foundation of dignity. Giancarlo told me that it felt really good to be part of a team again, and so he stepped back onto the field. He also confided that he knew Papa was watching, and would have been proud.

And indeed he would have, for as we've seen, Giancarlo did not distinguish himself with slugging percentages or a gold glove, but with the courage and grace to win, lose, and cast aside doubts that others tried to lodge within him. Two weeks after his mother had revealed the teasing of the other boys, I contacted Giancarlo's coach again to see if the situation had been managed, or perhaps had cleared itself naturally. I was rather startled by his reply.

"You should have seen it. Giancarlo stepped to the plate in the final inning last night and drove in the winning run with a walk-off line drive into the outfield. His teammates practically carried him off the field." I'd be willing to bet that he took a confident forward step into his swing.

It would be appealing to stop at this climactic event, the culmination of decisions and dignity and courage, tossed in with a bit of athletic prowess. A walk-off base hit is one of the grandest spectacles in all of sports, because the entire game swings just once with the bat. By its own definition, it is the finale. Game over, everyone walks off the field, stuffs gear into their bags, and goes home. But Giancarlo's hit that night was not the end of his story. There was a three-part coda to follow.

I was throwing batting practice one afternoon a few weeks later in the anteroom of the town's baseball complex, when I noticed a gaggle of boys merrily strolling and lolling into the adjacent cage and tossing their equipment lazily about, waiting for their coach. They were laughing, joking with each other, losing themselves on a warm afternoon in full baseball regalia. Their game was probably an hour away, and the furthest thing from their minds at the moment. Whether they knew it or not, I recognized this immediately as one of the most competitive advantages in all of sports. They were loose. More important, however, than the subcutaneous confidence that results from such limbering of the minds, is the inherent attraction to one another that follows. In religion it is known as fellowship. In music it is known as harmony. In baseball it is known as a team. At the heart of the laughter, leading both the applause and ready with the next one-liner, was Giancarlo. He hadn't just helped win a dramatic game, but with his wit, good nature, and determination, he was emerging in a role that he might not have expected, but one which his grandfather could probably have foretold. Giancarlo was becoming a leader. I nodded a friendly hello and smiled broadly as I returned to tossing balls. I wanted to ask him about his hit, but the time wasn't right.

Later, when we were writing to each other, I did. I asked him what it felt like to knock a game-winning hit out of the infield. In my life of playing baseball in one form or another as a kid and as an adult, I have amassed a grand total of one walk-off hit. I've had plenty of fine moments, and plenty of very humbling attempts at fine moments, but only one walk-off hit. Giancarlo knows the feeling, but true to a character forged by generations, and by timeless hours more precious than any regimen of practices, he answered as if Papa were standing right beside him:

"I felt really proud of my achievement, but I also felt that any one of my teammates could have done what I did. And I was really proud of them when they made good plays because we were all part of the same team. In that particular game they were all happy for me and voted to give me the game ball. The ball is on a special stand on my bedroom dresser, and I smile and think of my great coaches and my teammates every time I see it. I'll be on other teams in the future, I'm sure, but that moment will always stay in my mind." And his words gave me pause. I, too, have a game ball proudly displayed at home. We were down two runs in the bottom of the last inning of a semifinal game, with two outs, and I stepped up to bat with the bases loaded. With a 1–1 count, I laced the ball into center field and drove in the two tying runs, and we won the game on a walk-off hit when the next batter hit the ball into the same spot and drove home the remaining runner on third base. When I look at my game ball, I hear the climax of Beethoven's Ninth and a chorus of fifty-thousand imaginary fans crescendoing into "Freude, shöner Götterfunken . . ." (yes, I hear it in German) as I swing the bat in the slow motion highlight reel of my own fancy. Giancarlo looks at his game ball, and he thinks of his coaches, and his teammates.

And so for these reasons, it came as no surprise when I received word late in the season that Giancarlo had been nominated as a finalist for one of our town's most prestigious sports awards. In

January of the previous year, a twelve-year-old boy in town named Eric Green died very suddenly of a cardiac arrhythmia associated with hypertrophic cardiomyopathy. He was an avid baseball and lacrosse player, Boy Scout, and a jazz trumpeter, and peers and adults noted his sportsmanship and good will toward his teammates. In the words of a fellow coach and friend of mine who knew Eric very well, "Eric was a polite and friendly kid. In neighborhood games and organized sports he was inclusive and a magnet for other kids: when he was involved there were simply more happy kids in the game. He was a leader by example, a natural athlete who may not have been the best player on the field but always made his team better. Eric was also a good student and an excellent musician, but his defining characteristic was his enduring goodness."

Eric's brother, Alex, offered the following tribute to his brother, his "best friend," in an essay he wrote: "Eric treated everybody that he knew with respect. He respected our parents by never starting arguments with them. He also respected his teachers, coaches, and Scout leaders by working hard and trying his best. In addition, he also respected his peers. For example, although Eric was one of the better players on his team in lacrosse, he would frequently pass to other players to give them a chance to assist in a play or score. Eric showed courtesy to students at his school as well. One boy in Eric's grade was born deaf but received a cochlear implant in preschool. However, (his) speech remains more difficult to understand than a typical child. Eric took the time to stop, listen, and talk with him while they were in the school hallways."

Eric's coach in his final year of playing baseball often asked him to recite the Little League pledge before the games, and left a plaque with the pledge in the family's mailbox after Eric's death. Eric not only read the pledge, he lived it:

I trust in God
I love my country
And will respect its laws.
I will play fair
And strive to win
But win or lose
I will always do my best.

In honor of Eric's short but dignified life, the town now presents each year the Eric Green Sportsmanship Award to the Little League player who most clearly carries Eric's spirit forward. One player is nominated from each team in the age group where Eric played his last season, the eleven- and twelve-year-old boys (our town's "Major Leagues"). Giancarlo received his team's nomination. I happened to be out of town on the day that the nominees were presented to the assembled crowd during the season finale, and so I missed the presentation that I would have liked to have witnessed. The award went to another player who was equally deserving of the honor and who had played with Eric on a championship team of fifth graders when Eric pitched four innings. I can confidently imagine that Giancarlo was the first to shake his hand. And once again, I set aside my own pen in deference to the eloquence of this young ballplayer, for when I asked him how it felt to receive the nomination, he replied:

"I felt really bad that a kid my age had to die for this award to be invented. His family must be so sad, because everything I heard about Eric sounded like he was the greatest kid. I would have liked to have him as a friend. I also said that I wasn't sure that I deserved to be nominated for the award because I just did for my grandfather what any kid would do. It wasn't doing anything special. I also felt that being supportive of my teammates and cheering them on was what the game was all about, and again, I wasn't doing anything special. The whole team could have been nominated."

I am quite sure that Giancarlo would have been Eric's friend. And I believe that he would have memorialized him with the eloquence you have come to expect from him. He knows what it is to escort another person beyond this life with a strong hand. There was no Beethoven's Ninth as a backdrop to the honor bestowed by the award nomination. Barber's Adagio might have been Giancarlo's backstop through this experience, a piece that begins with despair, rises toward hope, and culminates in a tumult of emotion eclipsed by experience. I imagine both Papa and Eric removing their caps in reverence to Giancarlo's magnanimous words.

Like all athletes, baseball players set goals for themselves, and Giancarlo had been no exception. When his comeback season had finished, I returned to the misty Sunday morning that had first brought us together, and I recalled the unusual goal he had claimed as his own. It had not been to achieve a certain batting average, nor to become the star shortstop or relief pitcher. It had not been to win a game with a timely hit, to win a championship, or to win any sort of award or personal recognition. His goal was to win friends, classmates he would see in the hallways and across the classroom in the fall. They would share nods and smiles born from the shared experience of competing together and depending on one another.

And so, after the season was over and the school year had begun, I had two final questions for Giancarlo about his experience, and I asked with some trepidation because I had no idea how he might reply, or even if he would reply. The first question was simply whether or not he had achieved his goal—had he walked into school on the first day in September and found any friendly, famil-

iar faces from the ball field. I considered the possibility that even if
the answer was "no," he probably would not have regretted playing
ball, but the experience would have been a book on a shelf rather
than a story still unfolding. He replied,

> I was a new kid in school this September but it was easier than I
> thought because I did see the faces of kids I knew. I knew some
> kids from a Montessori school I went to from first to fourth
> grade, plus my baseball team kids, and I even recognized some
> faces of kids I had played from other teams. It was actually an
> awesome and comfortable first day.

In the legendary words of one of baseball's most beloved voices,
Mel Allen, "How about that!" Giancarlo had a good first day of
middle school in a new town because he had joined a baseball
team.

And then I asked the second question. I don't quite know precisely where it came from or why I even asked it. It was somewhat
disjointed, and it could have been, in retrospect, confusing or even
upsetting for Giancarlo. I asked it and immediately wanted to swal-
low the words, but decided instead to entrust them to his maturity.
He had been gracious enough already to share with me, a man not
much more than a stranger, some of the most profound places in his
young heart. And though, by his own accounts, neither his actions
nor decisions were ever as extraordinary as I saw them to be, I was
afraid that the question would somehow diminish in his own mind
all that had happened. Instead, his answer explained everything.

"Can you think of anything in common between the time you
spent in the hospital with your grandfather, and the time you spent
on the baseball field with your new friends?"

"This one is tough, but maybe this answer will be ok for you.
When I was with my grandfather, I was really only there to be with

him. I didn't think of school, I didn't think of summer camp, I didn't think of my friends. I only thought of Papa, of all the cool things we had done together, of what we experienced together. I thought of how lucky I was to have known him and that his blood and my blood were the same. When I played on the team, I didn't think of school or summer camp or vacation or anything else. I was all about the game, my teammates and my coaches. That's the thing you have to do, you have to be totally into whatever or wherever you choose to be, or what's the point?"

Giancarlo may one day be a genetic scientist who finds a way to press back against the phantom disease that took his grandfather's life, but not his name. Or he might perform at the Metropolitan, and like his mother and father, choose the arts as his way of broadening the lives of others. Whatever he chooses, he will be all in. For now, I was thrilled last week to see that he has signed up for another year of baseball.

ACKNOWLEDGMENTS

Without teammates, none of these stories would have been possible and so my hat is forever off to all of you (and I mean forever—recent knee reconstruction means that my playing days are fading). The genesis of this book was *The Season* with the Sunset Café softball team, and to each of you I offer thanks for your friendship and for never judging me by my foot speed. And to be perfectly honest, the luster of any good teammate is accentuated by the quality of our opponents, so to them, too, I tip my hat and raise my glass.

Thanks to Michael Steere of Down East Books for recognizing that these stories could be told, and to both Michael and Joe Miller for your editorial advice and help in crafting these ideas into a book. I'd take both of you in a pickup game any time.

It is my father Merold to whom I attribute my lifelong love of writing. He built a study in my childhood home with books stacked neatly from floor to ceiling on makeshift boards supported by rough old bricks. The pride that he and I share in his own philosophical works is no small source of my own inspiration. And it was my mother Carol who showed me throughout life that profound beauty may be found anywhere, in anything, or anybody—

even a sandlot. And then my sister Karla taught me how to laugh at myself—usually by laughing at me, too. The spirit and tone of these pages are from the wellspring of our shared lives.

I thank my children, Ben and Ellie, for weaving in and out of these pages with the beginnings of their own stories, and for graciously letting me coach their baseball and soccer teams. Together we learn the levels of the games, and wait for our next great story. And Sharon, thank you. I am proud to be raising these children with you.

Words are inadequate to convey the gratitude and admiration I have for the parents of other children who have found their way into these pages. Thank you to Suzanne Heinlen Green, mother of Eric Green, for whom our town's baseball sportsmanship award is named. You have shared your friendship and the story of the loss of your son in a way that perpetuates his spirit of good will. And to Laura and Jim, Giancarlo's parents, you have opened your family to me and to our readers in a way that shows how dignity begins in youth and is everlasting. To all of you, if nothing else in this book endures, I hope that readers will remember the character of Giancarlo and Eric, your sons. I know I will.

To Giancarlo, I thank you for the time you spent sharing your story and your voice with me in very personal terms, and for finding the courage to pick up a bat and return to a game you love on that drizzly Sunday morning. More than that, I thank you for reminding me that however ordinary or extraordinary a game may be, it is only a crescendo or diminuendo in a much more profound symphony.

Several teammates and wonderful friends have encouraged me during the retelling of the stories we shared. To Kevin, Jim, and Duke, I thank you for showing me what could be accomplished and for enjoying the folly and grandeur along the way to realizing it. We made every game matter.

To Katie, Jamal, Abosi, and my friends from Burundi. May our memories of Thanksgiving football become a small chapel in the remembrance of a country and the spirit of its people.

Many others have read initial drafts of these stories and have encouraged me in their telling, and helped to refine them. Many names already listed may be counted among my initial reviewers. To these, I fondly add Mark, Spandana, Larry, Dave, and Lisa. To Mrs. Rocker, thank you for putting the pen in my hand. And to Ms. Brylka, thank you for reading.

And to whomever it was who sold me that first red baseball for $3.99, I owe you one. And lastly, to the Sunset Café in Cambridge, thanks for sponsoring our team, for feeding us, and for celebrating all the highs and lows. Those were good times.

—Kirk

BIBLIOGRAPHIC NOTES

I drew upon a number of sources while compiling the recollection of these stories. Most of the telling came from my own memory of events, but was enhanced by personal interviews with participants, and various sundry references in books or radio and television that have stayed with me through the years. I'll give itemized credit where it is due below, by chapter, and the rest can be blamed on my memory. In addition, I offer my hearty thanks or apologies to Dr. Seuss, Henry Wadsworth Longfellow, Edgar Allen Poe, Lewis Carroll, and Ernest Thayer, who probably never knew they would inspire such adaptations or quothing's of their finest poetical works, and are probably glad not to have known. Next time I am at the Wayside Inn in Sudbury, Massachusetts (the famed historic site about which the tellings of Longfellow's *Tales of a Wayside Inn* were concocted), I will raise a pint in his honor. It is just a ten-minute drive from my house, and I visit every few months as long as the recreationist fife and drum corps is not practicing within the confines of the small tavern room, which they do. Back to the point at hand, and not the pint in hand, in various chapters I have offered modernized renditions of Longfellow's "Paul Revere's Ride" (from "Tales of a Wayside Inn"), Poe's "The Raven," Carroll's "Jabberwocky," Dr. Seuss's (Theodor Seuss Geisel) "The Grinch Who Stole Christmas," "and Thayer's "Casey at the Bat," all for the worse, and not the better.

Home Court Advantage: The facts and statistics about the NCAA Men's Basketball Tournament from 1997–2014 were compiled from my own notes taken during each year's tournament on my bracket sheets. After the first or second round of the tournament, I stop checking my guesses for the office pool and focus instead on documenting unique aspects about the individual games or that year's tournament as a whole. I owe the research behind many of the facts to the staff at CBS Sports, because it has been in watching and listening to the CBS broadcasts very attentively, sometimes compulsively, that I have gleaned this collection of remarkable achievements, coincidences, and veritable oddities. I also owe a debt of gratitude to Tim Kurkjian, the ESPN baseball commentator who finds as much glee in amassing his personal collection of extraordinary baseball trivialities as I do with basketball. His work has been no small inspiration to my own. Lastly, I owe a debt to the Monty Python comedy group (don't we all?) for their 1975 movie *Monty Python and the Holy Grail*. The reference in the chapter is one of the movie's many quotables.

Thanksgiving Football: I learned almost everything I know about the tragic history of Burundi from the book, *From Bloodshed to Hope in Burundi: Our Embassy Years during Genocide*, written by U.S. Ambassador Robert Krueger and his wife, Kathleen Tobin Krueger, with a foreword by Archbishop Desmond Tutu. It was published by the University of Texas Press in 2007. It has been through efforts of people such as these that the horrific stories of

East African genocide have received more attention than they did initially, when most of the world stood by and then turned away. My association with the Burundian family offered only a tangential glimpse into their violent and fearful history. I knew them as neighbors in their new country, but I am indebted to those such as the Kruegers who knew people like this family as neighbors in their own country.

The Season: I find it remarkable that the bibliography for this chapter includes Mike Krzyzewski, Adam Sandler, and Lisa Simpson, but there it is. The quotations from Mike Krzyzewski ("Coach K"), head basketball coach at Duke University, are found on pages 148 and 184 of his book *Leading with the Heart: Coach K's Successful Strategies for Basketball, Business, and Life*, published by Warner Books in 2000. In another place on the literary spectrum is Adam Sandler's comedy album *Shhh . . . Don't Tell*, on the Warner Brothers label, where the Gay Robot made his debut in 2004 (the year before he became our mascot). Lastly, the quip from the animated character Lisa Simpson of *The Simpsons* television show about the universality of having a nemesis is one of her classics. The show was created by Matt Groening, and aired on Fox television.

All of the simulated quotations from Kurt Gowdy and/or Vin Scully are just that—simulated. Nothing that I attribute to them was actually said by them, as far as I know, but their voices crackling over the old transistor radio in the garage or at the barber shop are part of baseball's great allure, so I attribute the tone of those imagined quotes to the thousands of games they actually covered.

And of course, the final line in the chapter is Al Michaels's famous call of the 1980 Olympic Hockey game between the United

States and the Soviet Union, the "Miracle on Ice," played on February 22, 1980, and aired on the ABC television network.

Magic Ball: The story of Armando Gallaraga was recounted from the vivid memory in my mind of watching that game live on television. I will never forget it.

The Timing Pattern: The references and quotations from Norman Maclean are taken from two of his writings. First is the book that I consider to be among the finest ever written, *A River Runs Through It*, published by the University of Chicago Press in 1976. Second is a collection of his writings and letters published posthumously, entitled, *The Norman Maclean Reader*, also published by the University of Chicago Press, this time in 2008. The C.S. Lewis quotation is excerpted from his novel, "The Lion, The Witch, and the Wardrobe," first published in 1950 by HarperCollins Publishers, and found on page 170 of the HarperTrophy edition.

Swing . . . and a Drive: Most of the baseball lore embedded in this chapter is from personal experience, and simply being a fan and absorbing the monuments of the game. I credit the neurons in my brain with tracking the walk-off home runs in playoff history. Clearly, they understand that these memories are more important than phone numbers or social security numbers or birthdays or names of colleagues. Many of the famous home run calls from television and radio commentators also dwell within my memory, but can be found online (with many others that are equally entertaining) at such sites as:

• www.baseball-almanac.com/quotes/quohomer.shtml

- bleacherreport.com/articles/1234709-ranking-the-best-home-run-calls-in-baseball

I also credit the hours upon hours that I have spent as a child watching Cubs games on WGN and as an adult watching Red Sox games on NECN with intimate knowledge of Harry Caray's and Don Orsillo's charming idioms.

The book I mention early in the chapter by Boston Sportswriter Dan Shaughnessy is entitled *Senior Year: A Father, A Son, and High School Baseball*, published by the Houghton Mifflin Company in 2007.

All In: The Little League Pledge can be found on the back of any Little League Handbook. It was written by Peter J. McGovern in 1954, and first appeared in *Little Leaguer Magazine* in 1955. The accounts of Giancarlo, Eric Green, and Eric's brother Alex were obtained through personal interviews with the families and various coaches in our town, whose names will remain private. To them, I am indebted, and in awe.